D1297498

THE SOUL DOCTOR

BY

CHARLES REED ZAHNISER

ROUND TABLE PRESS, INC.
NEW YORK 1938

PRINTED IN THE UNITED STATES OF AMERICA
BY CORNWALL PRESS, INC., CORNWALL, N. Y.

CONTENTS

FOREWORD

PROBLEMS of adjustment of personality and life situations are everywhere to the fore in present-day thinking. Along with those of social reconstruction, they are dominating the new fields of scientific inquiry in which there is now emerging the more adequate science of human nature, which must follow the great advances of the last century in the science of physical nature if our traditional culture is to endure.

In former times this was considered the particular field of religious agencies. Today it has been entered by many others: medical, educational and social, to say nothing of exploiters and charlatans. But this does not mean that the Church has retreated from the field as no longer within its responsibility. On the other hand, the whole swing of religious thinking is increasingly away from a pulpit-centered conception of its function in terms of the delivery of a message, to one of a clinical task in the conserving of spiritual life and the health of the soul.

This book is a mosaic word picture of such a clinical parish ministry. It consists largely of true stories from life, case histories, modified in form and location so as to prevent identification, but unchanged in any features of social or psychological import. All of them are drawn from the experience of the writer and his former students and others with whom he has been associated. The church and the minister around whom the story is built are, of course, fictitious.

The presentation rests on two convictions: that adequate personality adjustment must always include one's cosmic relations and therefore be religious, and that no church or minister can measure up to present-day responsibilities, and continue to have a place in the going social order without affording services to unadjusted human souls such as these pages are intended to depict. Written in non-technical language, it is put forth in the hope that it may be of help both to the minister in enriching his work for individuals, and to persons in distress who might find help in enlightened religious experience.

C. R. Z.

Boston University.

THE SOUL DOCTOR

I

THE ODYSSEY OF A MINISTER

THE Reverend Mortimer Alison was bewildered. Yes, bewildered; that was the proper descriptive word. Not disheartened nor discouraged, for his strong virile Christian faith in a God who was all-powerful and a Heavenly Father with love strong beyond comprehension, would not allow him to feel or to think in terms of discouragement. But he was bewildered; yes, he would have to admit bewilderment as he honestly faced the facts in his own situation.

It was now two years since he had taken charge of Old Second Church. He had come with a conviction that God had called him to the pastorate of this famous old church, on whose membership rolls hitherto there had been such great multitudes of people, so many Christian leaders in the community, city and nation, and he had come with high hopes of again making it a power, as it had been in its illustrious past. Two years, he felt, was long enough for him to see some tangible evidences of the results for which he had so confidently hoped and so earnestly labored. He did not forget that he had been warned when he was considering the call to become pastor of Old Second, that there was no future for it in its present location, that the only sensible thing to be done, in case he should become pastor, was to sell its valuable present location and to start anew in some up-and-coming suburb where the church would find people of prestige who would appreciate its messages and so would again become a power in the spiritual life of the city.

"But," Alison remembered he had protested, "there are more people living there than ever before, so why should the church leave?"

"Yes," his would-be advisers replied, "but what kind of people are they?"

"The kind for which Jesus Christ died!"

"Oh, yes, but you can't reach them. It's a degenerate community."

Well, what of that? A "degenerate community" they said. What if it was? Was not the gospel he had been called to proclaim intended for spiritual degenerates? Was not its crowning glory in the regeneration of the degenerate? Was not his omnipotent God equal to such a challenge as that? Such pessimism had seemed to him only a challenge to his faith. To move away for such a reason would be to surrender his faith in the whosoever-will gospel to which he had consecrated his life. That very advice had settled the question with him. If he were to come, Second Church must stay!

And stay it did. But now, after the passing of these two years, where were the evidences of the spiritual regeneration he had envisioned? Where were the results to justify what he had done? Mortimer Alison was bewildered.

The study in which he had been seated was in a quiet nook to one side of the pulpit in the rear of the old church, somewhat secluded from the street and sheltered from the noises of its everyday life. He rose from his mahogany swivel chair, paced back and forth for a time between the narrow walls, then opened the door and looked about over the vacant seats of the empty auditorium. It had seemed almost as deserted yesterday during the service when he had preached from the pulpit and had looked out over the relatively few faithful members scattered so widely about among the rows of many empty pews which years ago had been filled with worshipers. He could recall from memory where nearly every one of those faithful few had been seated yesterday. Verily, he had felt yesterday as his voice resounded among those many, many vacancies, that he was pretty much a voice crying in the wilderness!

Passing down one of the aisles through the silent auditorium, he walked out into the vestibule and peered through the small Gothic-crowned vestibule window, from which there was a clear view of the street and its crowded structures. There was the array of houses he had so often surveyed before; houses, houses everywhere and all of them dwellings of human souls his church was set to serve, souls hungry to know the real meaning of life, longing for assurances of security and understanding and grounds for faith and hope. True, some of the houses had lost something of their former attractiveness, some pretentious ones of yesterday were now converted into rooming houses with all the markings of their new rôle, but what of that? That meant there were now twenty, thirty or more people living where only a single family had enjoyed life before. Others had been torn down and replaced by the clustered cubicles of present-day abiding places graciously called apartments, but that, also, had been the means of bringing more families under the shadow of Old Second. Business, too, had crowded in on the street faced by the church, and dwellings had been remodeled with store fronts on their first floors. But Alison knew that they were mistaken who assumed this meant there were no people living there. For back of these stores and on the upper floors were again people who found there the only homes they had, men busy making a living, women burdened with household cares, children hampered for room to play, all of them needing the very spiritual ministries Second Church was intended to give, and yet many of them, Alison had reason to believe, attending no church whatever.

Yes, there were people living there, more people than ever before. If there was need of a church there in the days when this beautiful church edifice had been erected amidst the homes of the affluent, why was it not more needed now? Why should it surrender and move away?

He had asked that question many times before. But today it led on to another. For he faced the fact that despite this increase in population and despite the greater spiritual need and distressing spiritual hunger which he sensed on every side, very few of these people had been in Second Church yesterday; more than that, very few of them had ever responded to any of its approaches. Yesterday, his voice sounded over mostly vacant pews, while within a five minute walk of the church had been people enough to fill it to capacity who had gone nowhere to church. He had succeeded in keeping the church in the community, but he had not succeeded in getting the community into the church to any very gratifying extent.

From the houses, his eyes now turned to the many men, women and children on the street; hurrying people, he wondered why and to what destination; slowly dragging people, as though something had either drained their strength or left them without a goal; manifestly thoughtless people, mostly youngsters, tripping along with an unconcern or superciliousness so evidently superficial that he could not but be reminded of the proverbial butterfly; hardened, belligerent people, whose cruel exteriors he well knew were but vain compensations for the poverties of their own discomfited inner selves; anxious, distressed, disheartened people, whose countenances said all too plainly that they had gone beyond the bewilderment in which he now found himself, had gone on to where bewilderment bordered on despair. As he looked at them, his heart went out in a familiar cry; "O, Jerusalem, Jerusalem! How often would I have gathered thy children together even as a hen doth gather her brood under her wings and ye would not!"

Alison turned and slowly retraced his steps back into his study.

"And ye would not!" Why? God knows I have honestly tried. God knows my people have stood faithfully by me. God knows I have brought sermon messages of the very kind these people are needing. I know I have kept my messages abreast of the thinking of my times, and I have been dealing with the felt problems and needs of my times. Why, then do they not come to receive? What is wrong with my gospel that it does not appeal?

That last thought arrested him. "My gospel?" That Christian gospel I fully accepted and made my own when I committed my life to this ministry, am I losing faith in that? His mind flashed back to a scene in his boyhood home, when he had returned as a senior in college, thinking to surprise his mother by telling her of a transforming spiritual experience when, like Wesley, he had felt his heart strangely warmed within him, and he had determined to enter the ministry of the Church. But the surprise had been his own. For his mother had manifested none whatever. Instead she had very quietly said, "I knew it would come. Son, I gave you to that work before you were an hour old!"

He recalled also how his heart had been fired by an unquestioning confidence in the dynamic quality of that gospel he had set himself to deliver. "The power of God unto salvation!" That exultant confidence of Paul he had made his own, a full confidence that this gospel can lift us out of everything that hampers and hinders and corrupts and befouls and destroys, and into everything that makes life true, beautiful, good and satisfying. The adequacy of his gospel; no, as he meditates now upon it with maturer experience, he cannot doubt that. The years between have taught some sweet, some bitter lessons, but none more convincing than this; that there is ample adequacy in the gospel of Christ. Paul was right; not only "In him was revealed all the fullness of the godhead embodied," but also "In him ye are made full!" There is nothing lacking in our gospel.

For a long time that morning, Mortimer Alison sat musing. More than he realized, the fire within him burned. Two facts loomed large before him: the manifest spiritual needs of the people about, and the eternal values of the gospel with which he was entrusted; there the need, here the supply; there the soul sickness, here the remedy; the two not relating themselves together. Where is the fault? Of course, it would be easy to blame it on the people; to say they ought to come, they ought to seek what I know they need. But Alison could not bring himself to do that. He knew that business men do not find such an alibi for themselves. If people do not come to their marts to buy, they do not waste time blaming the public; rather they examine their own sales program to find wherein they are failing to attract customers. Precisely so it should be with the Church. We are salesmen for Almighty God, to offer in His name what is of greater value than aught else a human soul can enjoy. If people pass us by unheeding, it is for us to ask wherein we are failing to attract.

But wherein are we failing? For that question he found no ready answer. He realized it was crucial. Perhaps in this lay the real source of his bewilderment. Alison faced the question honestly. He had never been one to find alibis for his own shortcomings in the deeds of others. But, on the other hand, he was honest with himself also, and he would not accuse himself of that which his intelligence told him was not true. And so, as he faced the situation, he knew that the fault was not in a lack of earnest and devoted effort either on his own part or that of his people in the church. He knew the meaning of real Christian consecration to an enterprise, and he knew that it would be unjust to charge the evident failures in Second Church to lack of honest devotion on the part either of himself or of his fellow workers. The cause must be found elsewhere. But where and what? Alison pondered long on that.

The problem was not one to be easily solved in a day. Alison prayed much over it. He had no hesitancy about that. It was his practice to do precisely this with all of his problems, then wait patiently for the clarified convictions which experience had convinced him God would help him achieve.

In the meantime, the period for his annual vacation drew nigh. Alison decided he would spend it in New York, presumably our most intensely urbanized community, studying some of the typical areas there from which, as urbanization proceeded, the churches generally retreated and ultimately withdrew. He would try to find what kind of agencies and programs showed promise of reaching the people there. He was fortunate in becoming located in a settlement, and securing the friendship and help of a welfare worker of wide experience in the surrounding communities. He spent the entire vacation period in going about visiting the people, noting the character of current social changes, comparing the policies and programs of the retreating churches and those of other agencies at work in these communities. As he did so, he was concerned chiefly with the fact that the churches were retreating, and social agencies were coming in. He was seeking the reason for this. Manifestly, the churches retreated because they despaired of reaching the people, and the other agencies came in because they had confidence they could reach them. But why did the one despair and the other have confidence? What did the social agencies have which was lacking in the churches? Alison never doubted that the churches did have in their gospel a spiritual dynamic that cannot be excelled, but what did the social agencies have which gave them ground for confidence, even without a religious emphasis? More and more, Alison found himself saying, they have a technique. Then came his inspiration: *"Learn from their technique."*

Learn from their technique! Alison went home with that challenge sounding in his soul. Not learn *their* technique; he was too experienced in life to make that error. He knew that the actual techniques of one art cannot be bodily transferred to another. He who tries to ape another attains only apish results. He had no intention of transforming Second Church into a social agency or taking over the work that social agencies are particularly fitted to do. But he did propose to develop policies and programs in the work of the church, with techniques of their own, embodying certain principles which he had become convinced made for entree and effectiveness in the work of the social agencies. These principles he found centering in and pretty much circling about what the social worker called "case work." In variant forms, he found case work to be both the means of approach and the means of carrying through, on which practically all of the progressive social agencies put their main dependence. Why, then, should we not develop a program of case work in the Church?

Case work in the parish program: the more Alison allowed that thought to develop, the more revolutionary he found it to be. From a place in the periphery, he found it more and more moving into the center of the working program now needed in Second Church. But to do case work meant a real revolution in his thinking about his own task also.

The Church primarily a case working agency? That involved a complete re-orientation of the whole conception of the ministry he had received in the theological seminary. There he was given to understand, as for that matter he had always understood, and as seemed to be understood by most Christian people, that the controlling function of the minister is the delivery of a message. He had been given to understand that he was to see himself in the succession of the prophets of old, commissioned to "stand forth in the midst and cry aloud!" He was to be in the community as one who had a "message" to deliver, and therefore his training was to be of a kind that would enable him to deliver that message effectively. He was to see his task as "evangelical," the bearing of a message of good news to a sinful and suffering human race, as an "evangelist," a bearer of a message of hope to sinful men. He had thrilled to the picture in a favorite gospel song,

> "I am a stranger here, within a foreign land,
> My home is far away upon a golden strand;
> Ambassador to be, from lands beyond the sea,
> I'm here on business for my King!
> This is the 'message' that I bring!"

This conception of the minister's chief function is evident also in the term usually applied to him in popular parlance: "The Preacher." People generally think of a minister primarily as a man standing in a pulpit delivering an oration. Indeed, that was pretty much what Alison himself had thus far thought himself to be. One reason, his friends told him, why they had encouraged him to go ahead with his purpose of becoming a minister, was that he had oratorical gifts. The seminary was always on the lookout for a young man talented in that way. Then they had trained him to be effective in the techniques of public address. They schooled him in those aspects of mass psychology on which the skilful orator plays to obtain his desired effects. They taught him the subtle arts of rhetoric in order that he might phrase and illustrate his "message" in ways that would capture attention, stimulate imagination, and arouse emotional reactions towards the ends desired. Then they gave him to understand that his success in the ministry would be appraised largely in terms of his attainments in these arts.

That explained also why his seminary training included so much emphasis on biblical exegesis; that along with the ideas of scriptural inerrancy then prevailing in his particular communion. For, if the minister's task was primarily the delivery of a message, and if that message was to be found in the original Hebrew and Greek in which were written "the scriptures of the Old and New Testaments, the only infallible rule of faith and practice," it became highly important that he should be expert in exegesis whereby the exact meaning of scripture might be ascertained and interpreted. It was all to make him an effective preacher.

But the Church as primarily a case working agency, and himself its head and director; that manifestly was something quite different. It meant an entirely different configuration for his ministry. Not that the preaching function was to be entirely dismissed, of course. It would still remain, but it could no longer assume to be the dominant interest to which all others should be adjunct and contributory. In the proposed new orientation, with case work to the fore, the dominant objective would be found in human needs to be met rather than in a message to be delivered, and preaching would appear as just one of the means whereby the minister would undertake to realize his Master's ideal, "that they may have life, and that they may have it more abundantly."

But should preaching not be allowed the central

place in the Christian program? The very structure of Second Church edifice seemed to suggest it. For there stood the pulpit in the midst, out in front of the altar and in front of the cross. Just why should it be there? This inquiry sent Alison to a renewed study of Church history, in which he found that this centrality of the pulpit was one of the side products of the Protestant Reformation. Prior to that time there were here and there great outstanding preachers like Savonarola and St. Benedict, and there was some preaching done generally, particularly by the missioners of the Church, but preaching as we know it was not thought of as central to the program nor was the minister called a "preacher." Rather, he was commonly called the "curé," the man who took care of souls. True he became also known as the "priest," charged with performing various sacerdotal functions in connection with which arose many of the abuses which led to the Reformation. But these abuses, Alison saw, should not obscure from us the loving ministries of many faithful men which conserved much of what was good in the Church and which gave them the popular name of "curé."

When the Protestant Reformation got under way, one of its most significant differentials was symbolized by the taking of the pulpit down from the side of the cathedral and pushing it out into the center of the sanctuary in front of the altar and in front of the cross. It was significant because it symbolized a pulpit-centered conception of the Christian enterprise. Perhaps this was a natural development. For Luther, Calvin and

Wesley were preeminently preachers. And the times were devoid of general education and of widely distributed literature. Instruction was of necessity largely given by word of mouth, which would naturally place a strong emphasis on preaching. With the passing of time the continuance of that conception produced quite generally a pulpit-centered Church program. Alison saw this had been notably true of Second Church. Just as the pulpit stood out as the central feature in their building, so their whole Church program was built around the Sunday morning service, and that service was built around the sermon with "opening and closing exercises."

As Alison mused over this situation, he had to confess to himself that the pulpit preeminence had probably been quite gratifying to his own vanity. It is but natural that one should enjoy the appreciative response of an audience and the personal prestige which such a pulpit emphasis affords. He was not sure that he had yet reached a place where he was willing to surrender this. But he did wish that Second Church would follow the present trend in so much of Protestantism to put the pulpit back in its original place at the side of the sanctuary, opposite the reading desk and away from its prominent position in front of altar and cross. At least he was sure he did not want to obtrude himself so much in front of what symbolized the sacrifice and service of his Lord and into fellowship in which our Lord calls us. It might not be possible to move Second Church pulpit just now, but one resolve he made and determined to carry out; he would at least do so in his own heart and program. From now on, by the grace of God, he would build his whole program around the effort to ascertain and meet the spiritual needs of the people in this community, and he would direct his pulpit work as one means to that end.

But when Alison undertook to elaborate such a reoriented program for his work, he quickly found that it was going to require skills and techniques for which his professional training as a minister had given him little preparation. Indeed, as he now looked back over his theological school training, he found only sparse scatterings of anything which would be of particular help here. As a protestant minister, he simply had not been trained for this kind of a job.

Fortunately, however, it so chanced that he had himself enjoyed some experiences in his own background which, while they had not been undertaken with ministerial duties in mind, did, nonetheless, stand him now in good stead as he faced this situation. While in college, he had become interested in applied psychology and sociology, particularly in psychotherapy and the psychological approach to the problems of behavior and the incidence of crime. He had continued this line of study in a personal way during his theological course, and had spent some time one summer in a psychopathic hospital as a student assistant to the social workers.

Following this he had a similar experience for a few weeks in a reformatory, where he worked with the psychologist and the chaplain, particularly among the young men looking forward to early parole. The work had deeply interested him, and in subsequent years in the pastorate, he had often cooperated with local social and correctional agencies, so that he had learned something of their viewpoints and techniques. He had really done considerable case work as a volunteer among them, but he had done this because of his personal interest, and he had not associated it particularly, even in his own thinking, with his church and ministry.

He realized now that this background gave him an equipment not enjoyed by every minister for undertaking what he was now trying to formulate. Perhaps this past experience, along with his recent observations in New York, had much to do with the direction of his present thinking concerning a Church program. Perhaps, even more, in the providence of God it was precisely that he should be prepared to pioneer in the type of program he was now trying to formulate, that his history had led through these experiences which had given him an unusual equipment for it. However that might be, he proposed now to put all this to use in inaugurating his new program.

Several months had elapsed since that morning when Alison had frankly faced and begun to study his own bewilderment. He had reached a place where the general outlines of the new program for his church work, which the reorientation in his thinking required, had become quite clear. Like Abraham, he had responded to a call and gone out not knowing whither he went, but with faith that his Odessey would be directed into a more effective form of service. Like Abraham, too, he realized now that he had reached the place to which he had journeyed, but it was one in which there was little yet mapped or charted, and he must needs continue to dwell in tents of easily shifted locations while continued explorations revealed in more detail the lines to be pursued. The time had now come when he should interpret to his fellow workers in the Church what he was convinced was God's call to him and them for a new pioneering enterprise in the process of God's economy through the ages. Manifestly the kind of program he now saw necessary was one in which they would be participating. And to that end it must be interpreted to them. That was the next thing to be done. But so far as Alison's own mind and soul were concerned, the Odyssey had arrived.

II

THE CHALLENGE

IT WAS a bright Sunday morning in the autumn with just enough chill in the air to be stimulating. Mortimer Alison sat in his pulpit facing what he realized was a relatively full attendance of his people, back now from their summer vacations and ready for a new year together in the Church. Their numbers seemed small in the spacious auditorium, but he knew they were true and believed in him. This was the day to which he had been looking forward when he would challenge them with his new program. Their presence and attitude cheered him. He had already talked over his plans with members of the official board and others of influence, and was assured of their sympathetic support. Yet he realized this support was in no small part because of their loyalty to him. Some of them he knew were bewildered by it all. Bewildered? Yes, that was the proper word. His mind flashed back many months to that Monday morning when he, too, was bewildered. Then for a moment he sat with closed eyes and saw again what he saw that morning as he gazed from the vestibule window on houses and people. The vision gave him strength. It was time for the sermon. He rose to speak.

"My friends and fellow-workers," he began quietly, "I am not going to preach a sermon from a text this morning. Rather, I propose to talk to you rather informally and quite frankly about our work together in this church and about some changes I hope we can make in our program. For I am frank to say to you that I am disappointed and dissatisfied. Not with your fellowship and support, for these have been all that could be desired. But I am disappointed with what we have been accomplishing among the people of this community and dissatisfied with our present outreach into it.

"I now think that this is because we have not been going about our work in the right way. Indeed, we have counseled very little together regarding the major features of our program, as you know. We inherited most of it from the practices those of earlier years found effective in their day, and we have naturally gone along in pretty much the same channels. But in the meantime the life situations in which we find ourselves have greatly changed and, despite the increased number of people living here, our own numbers are far below the congregations that assembled here in the days of our fathers. I am convinced our methods are out-moded and that the time has come when we should make some rather fundamental changes. I want, this morning, to suggest to you some changed approaches which seem to me imperative.

"It seems to me that this has to do basically with my own work. We have centered our program largely in my preaching. I confess I have gauged our progress in no small measure on the extent to which people come to hear my sermons. Now, I know, and so do you, that people simply are not going to churches today to hear sermons anywhere in the proportions of former days. The simple fact is that relatively few people go to hear sermons nowadays except church people. But I do not believe that need disconcert us. The same situation obtains in everything else; people do not go in large numbers to hear speeches on other things either. And after all, was it not to 'them that love the Lord' that the apostle addressed his plea that they 'forsake not the assembling of themselves together'? I have reached the place where I am no longer frightened over the fact that our preaching is likely to be limited to few others than our own people. I shall continue to preach and shall count it a privilege to do so.

"But I am convinced that this is not the whole, nor even the center, of the minister's work. And I am just as convinced that an effective church is not merely an audience brought together to hear a man make a speech. Rather it is a group of people working together in a common enterprise among whom the minister serves in a three-fold capacity, a trinity in himself, as it were. He indeed has a preaching task as I have already indicated, but he is to be also a physician of souls, and, of equal importance, he is to be a human engineer, an executive, supervising and directing the cooperative efforts of the group of people he has been called to serve. Now, it is in these last two aspects of my ministry that I feel I have fallen short, and that our program has been defective. So today, I am challenging you to enter with me into a new orientation of the program of our church; a program in which I will still preach, but it will be chiefly to you as workers together with me in our common enterprise; a program in which you will participate as partners in cooperative spiritual ministries for this community; a program in which we will undertake both to nurture the growth of normal spiritual life and to render clinical help to sick souls. It will be a program in the interest of spiritual life and health, in which we will try to be in every way as scientific as we expect the phsycian to be to whom we look for counsel in the physical nurture of our children and to whom we go for help in our bodily ills. In it we will think of this church building as the central operating station, from which we try to work out helpfully into the lives of the people of this community, with whatever kinds of ministry will make for the relief of distress of soul and for the making of life worthwhile. I do not ask you to respond to this challenge today. I ask you, rather, to meditate prayerfully on its implications during the coming week. Then a week from today I propose to set before you the type of program implied in a ministry to the health of souls in which I am inviting you to participate with me. Only thus can I see Second Church justifying itself in this community. But by such a program I am convinced it can achieve and arrive."

The greetings at the church door after the service were much as usual—too much as usual, throbbed Alison's burdened heart. How many of these people really understood?

At least, no one seemed offended. Principal Johnson of the local high school asked sagely in passing, "I wonder how you are going to implement that." Good old Mrs. Wetherby pressed his hand warmly and said, "Wonderful sermon!" But then, she always said that. He feared she had no idea what it was all about. Dr. Rogers stopped to talk a bit more. As a practicing physician in the community he caught much more of the implications and doubtless envisioned not a few cases in which such ministries might be highly helpful if skilfully done. "If skilfully done!" There was the question. Otherwise, it might easily be just too bad. "Well, we'll see," said Dr. Rogers. "I'll be interested in what you say next Sunday."

All in all, Alison felt encouraged. It takes time for new ideas to become an integral part of one's mental content. He would not unduly hurry.

The next Sunday found Alison ready for his effort to interpret and sell the proposed new program to his people. He felt also that they were somewhat ready for it. They had been given a week to think over the situation, a week in which their curiosity was aroused by his having explained so little and yet having quite evidently felt so deeply. His strategy in this had brought them this morning both curious and open-minded to hear what he had to propose.

Alison launched directly into his sermon. Two texts brought together furnished its basis by their juxtaposition: "I am come that they may have life, and that they may have it more abundantly." "As the Father hath sent me into the world, even so send I you!" "Here," said Alison, "is the Church's objective and commission; that men may be helped toward the enjoyment of a life abundant by an invigorating and enlightening experience of God in their lives. The Church indeed has a 'message' to deliver, a message of God so manifest in the Christ life that Jesus could truthfully say, 'He that hath seen me hath seen the Father!' The God character, the God dynamic, the God devotion to a mission, all these so manifestly imbuing the personality of Jesus that His life has become the paragon of history; God so made real in the minds of men, that in this fellowship one might find adjustment and peace and joy in living. This it was for which Jesus lived and died and for which He challenges us to follow in His steps! All this is no new thought to you this morning. You have heard it generally from this and other pulpits.

"But you have not seen it get across into the consciousness of multitudes in this community. Here we are, a little handful of people this morning, imbued with this idea. But this afternoon ten times our number will be seeking a satisfying abundance for life in the neighboring picture show; five times our number will do so tonight at the wrestling match in the arena. Let us be realistic this morning, and face the facts as they are. Our problem is, How shall we implement our message so that it will get across into the lives of these who vainly seek satisfactions elsewhere for yearnings which are really spiritual?

"I submit to you, that we can do so only by interpreting that message to each individual in terms of his own felt needs. They are the only ones that interest him, no matter how much you and I may think others are more important. It is there we must begin. It is a sick soul with which we are undertaking to deal, and we must begin with it as it is. But that means we must get to know it as it is. Ours is the task of a doctor of the soul, and as such we must be able to begin as does the physician of the body. You do not see the physicians trying to herd a lot of sick people into a meeting where a speech can be made telling them of the medicinal values of the various articles arrayed on drug store shelves and then issuing one prescription to them *en masse*. Yet precisely that has too commonly been our program in the Church. What I am now proposing is that we shall make the same intelligent approach in dealing with problems of spiritual health as they do with those that are physical. Now let me point out some of the specific changes this will entail in Second Church:

"First, it will be *Individualized*. We are not going to be concerning ourselves with any abstraction we might call 'the sinner.' Our concern is going to be with the discouraged man, the run-away girl, the swaggering youth, the distressed home, quarreling children, nagging wife, indifferent husband, right here in this community. All about us are show-window fronts of lives. Outwardly they are contented and care-free, but back of those carefully arranged fronts the skilled observer catches glimpses of spiritual squalor and disorder, uncouthness and discontent which unhappy souls try to conceal even from themselves. No two of them are alike, no two have like life situations, no two are wrestling with like combinations of demons. And no two of them are to be treated alike. I can no more prescribe for them together from this pulpit than could a physician for their bodily health. We must make our approaches to each person where he is and as he is.

"Second, it will begin with *Diagnosis*. We must have done with a spiritual therapy much akin to that of the patent medicine vendor who stands at a street corner making a speech about one bottle of dark brown liquid from which every hearer is advised to take three spoonfuls a day for anything from tuberculosis or cancer to insanity or bunions.

"Third, it will include the *Whole of Life*. William Booth was right when he began his effort to save the soul of a hungry man by filling his stomach. I am not surprised that many today, feeling keenly some social injustice under which they suffer, dub a religion which ignores the wrong or urges merely patient endurance, an 'opiate of the people.' Modern clinical psychology is showing us how necessary it is to deal with the whole of a personality and its entire life setting, if we would help that soul into enduring satisfaction. The only kind of a salvation that is going to interest people is one which helps adjust unhappy homes, baffled loves, frustrations, antagonism, anxieties, fears. John Wesley widened his gospel when he cried, 'The world is my parish!' We must widen it still more to include all of every life.

"Fourth, it will require a *Prolonged Process.* We now know that any conversion that amounts to much is never an isolated experience. There is back of it a long story of frustrations and visions of better things, there follows after it much of helpful cultivation and care. It is going to be necessary for us to take ample time to secure the confidence and trust of those with whom we deal. Often we will have to wait till some distressing or perplexing life situation makes the opportunity for spiritual ministry in a larger way. Often we will have to give time for seed to grow. Wise gardeners do not constantly dig up their seeds to see whether they have sprouted. Nor do they undertake to pluck corn while it is still in the blade. Wise case workers do not hurry.

"In all this we will be concerning ourselves as much with prevention as with cure. Just as modern medicine is first concerned with nurture of healthy growth and prevention of disease, so it must be ours to nurture high ideals and aspirations, spiritual resistances and reliances. This, of course, is going to require patience and skill on our part, skill in many cases beyond that of the average person in the Church. These skills it will be a particular responsibility of your pastor to provide or secure. I have weighed all this and realize the heavier loads it places upon me. But standing face to face with the spiritual needs about us and with a sense of what it means to be your minister, I dare do no less. Garibaldi once drew a line in the sand with his sword and said to his followers, 'On yonder side lie safety and food and home and friends, but slavery. On this side lie hunger and toil, danger and death, but free Italy! Choose each one of you on which side you will stand. But I stand here!' Can we today do less?"

Alison paused. Much of what he said had been carefully read from manuscript. For a moment he looked calmly and steadily into the eyes of his people. When he again spoke, it was with subdued, controlled emotion. "This is the program I propose. It is the only one I believe can be effective here. Into this I am ready to give all I have and am. I hope that it will seem likewise to you and that you will approve of its being undertaken and join me in making it real!"

The following week Alison rather kept away from his people. He wanted them to have more time in which to think through the implications of what he had proposed. He realized, too, that the sweeping changes of program which he had proposed could not but be somewhat bewildering to many of them. The very language he had used was much of it new and strange to that pulpit. There would needs be much more explaining and enlarging before he could go to them individually with specific proposals. But all that could come later.

Then something else happened.

Roy Bullard, whom Alison had known as a younger class man in college but who had since entered the ministry and was now a pastor in a small town church upstate, came into his study with an interesting story. He told how the church of which he was pastor still persisted in holding a second preaching service every Sunday evening, but with the attendance discouragingly small, often not over a dozen people. Bullard undertook to secure a larger attendance by announcing in advance some sensational topics. Recently he had announced that he would preach the following Sunday night on "The Biggest Sinner in Town!" Bullard said he had intended to base his sermon on the man in one of the Master's parables who hid his talent in a napkin, and to set forth the seriousness of the negative failures in life. But within a few days he had received no less than eight letters, some of them signed, most of them anonymous, all of them warning the preacher not to talk about them in his sermon!

Bullard was nonplused. Uncertain what to do, he went to consult an older minister, one who had been his frequent counselor. His friend said, "Man, you have the opportunity of your life!"

"Well tell me what to do," said Bullard. "I'm stuck!"

Together they talked the whole situation over and worked out both the plan and the sermon along lines suggested by the older minister. When Sunday evening came, Bullard was delayed by another engagement and one of the officials had opened the service for him. When he entered he faced an audience of a hundred and fifty people. It was time for the sermon and Bullard launched at once into his address.

He began by saying, "I'm going to take you people quite frankly into my confidence tonight. When I announced that topic, I intended to speak on our sins of omission, the commonest and often the most injurious of our wrong-doings. But since I announced the topic, I have received more than a half dozen letters, all from persons warning me not to talk about them tonight. Now, I'm going to talk to you on the basis of those letters.

"I'm not going to tell you what is in those letters. Nor am I going to say whether I know who wrote any of them, or whether I recognize any of the writers here tonight. I am going to treat those letters as confidences given to me as pastor of this church. There is one thing we must all admire about the Roman Catholic priesthood, no matter how much some of us may criticize some other things they do. All of us must admire the way they guard the secrets of the confessional. The priest would give his life before he would betray those confidences. Now, I feel very much the same way about confidences given to me as your pastor. And I want to say here and now, both to those who wrote the letters and to all the rest of you, that if at any time you have any problems in which you think I can be of help to you, I hope you will feel free to come to me about them. And I assure you I will keep your confidences as sacredly as does the Roman Catholic priest.

"But there is one thing written all over every one of those letters about which I do want to speak. That is, that every person who wrote such a letter is an unhappy soul. That letter was written because there is something in that person's life which, if I revealed it tonight, would not be approved by this community.

All these writers know that, and because of that they are not happy. I have no doubt that every one of them, if talking to me, would try to show that they were really right in the matter and the community wrong. And I might agree with them! But all that is incidental. The important fact is that they are unhappy souls tonight, and I wish I could help them.

"And now, there is something else I want to say to the rest of you. Many of you no doubt came here tonight, quite well satisfied I was not going to talk about you. And you have been moistening your lips, perhaps, in eager anticipation of some choice morsel of gossip about some neighbor you were going to enjoy. If that is true, let me suggest to you that perhaps you ought to get down on your knees before your God tonight and ask him whether you are not the biggest sinner in this town? Listen while I read." Then he read the passage in the eighth chapter of John about the woman taken in adultery and Jesus' treatment of her accusers.

Bullard said he never had such an experience in his previous ministry. The whole audience was deeply moved. It was a Methodist church, and the meeting ended in an old fashioned altar service.

Before nine o'clock the next morning no less than six persons had come to Bullard asking for conferences. Some of them were leading members of his church. They had revealed to him distressing burdens, harrowing inner conflicts right among his own people, of which he had previously had no idea.

The next Sunday morning, Alison briefly told Bullard's story in his own pulpit. Perhaps there were those among his people also, he suggested, who were feeling the need of a clinical ministry of the kind he had been proposing, and would like to consult him accordingly. It was only a passing comment given with quiet sincerity.

The results were much the same as had come to Bullard. One and another of his people came to Alison and quietly asked for appointments to discuss their own problems. As he made these appointments and then met these people in conference over their troubles, he realized that his clinical ministry had begun. Much of it was cut out for him for the present, right here among those close to him.

But he realized more than this. He realized also, that in thus accepting a clinical ministry for themselves, his people were accepting it also for the program of the church.

And he was content.

III

SISTERS THREE

Thelma

ALISON found his first case in his own home and on the day when he told Bullard's story.

Thelma was a young friend of Mrs. Alison in college days, now married, who had come to the city to spend the week-end with them. She had been at the church service and heard the Bullard story. After dinner as they sat in their parlor, she broached her problems. As she proceeded she became greatly agitated, threw herself onto a sofa and cried out her longing to die. Gradually the whole story came out. Alison faced his first challenge to prescribe for a suffering soul.

In this case, because of the unusual circumstance of Thelma being a personal friend of Mrs. Alison, it was all in her presence and the treatment was with her cooperation. Ordinarily this would not have occurred. Alison had already established an understanding with his wife that confidences brought to him as pastor were not to be shared with her unless there was some particular reason for so doing, usually in the way of her being asked to assist in the program for that person. And even in such cases, she would not expect to have more explanation than would be given to anyone else whose aid might be similarly sought. She understood that her position was quite like that of a physician's wife, who realizes that the confidences and secrets which come to her husband in a professional way are not her concern and that it would be entirely unethical for him to discuss them with her. Alison had also seen to it that his people understood this, so that they could come to him with their intimate problems assured that even she who was closest to him in mutual confidences did not expect and would not be permitted to share in the confidences of others which he might receive in this professional relation.

But with Thelma it was different. Mrs. Alison was her trusted friend through whom she found herself seeking counsel and help. So she was encouraged to go right on with her disclosures in the presence of Mrs. Alison. At the same time, Mrs. Alison did not forget that, after all, she was not the expert consultant, and so with a delicate feminine skill she did not presume to participate either in diagnosis or prescription. That was for him whose professional guidance was being sought.

At the time Thelma was twenty-nine years old, married five years, no children. Her husband, Will R., and herself were both active members of the church in the up-state town where they had grown up together. Both were college graduates, he partly trained for medicine. Both had been successful school teachers. He was the only son of a well-to-do farmer owning a fruit farm said to worth fifty thousand dollars. Thelma had considerable money of her own and was an only child. She had grown up in that town where her father was in business, had been somewhat pampered, was of delicate sensibilities but not considered "spoiled." Both were quite popular locally.

Thelma had been in ill health for some three years. After extended medical service she had undergone abdominal surgery which seems to have been largely exploratory. No serious organic trouble was discovered and she had experienced a rapid convalescence. But she had continued to complain of various pains. The present diagnosis, Alison surmised and later confirmed from other sources, was hysteria. The presumption, of course, would be that the ultimate cause, as usual with hysteria, was mental, probably an emotional conflict of some kind in which it was easily possible that religious factors should have a part. It seemed desirable, therefore, that she should uncover the whole situation to him. Understandingly and encouragingly he listened to her story, occasionally asking questions to direct her talk to things seeming to be important. He remembered a "Rule of Thumb" given him in a case work class at the University:

> *"Never be surprised, never be shocked,*
> *Never ridicule, never argue,*
> *Never pity, never blame,*
> *Always manifestly understand!"*

He would not only try to understand, he would try to make that fact plain also to Thelma. Nothing would go farther in the way of encouraging her to make a clean breast of whatever was in her mind, particularly what she might have hitherto concealed from others, even tried to conceal from herself. He would not blame her nor ridicule nor be shocked, for that would stop her frank disclosures. He would not pity nor argue, for either would only increase her neurosis by strengthening her inner conflicts. But he would "manifestly understand." As he did so, the whole story came out.

Following their marriage Will had attended medical school for a year and a half, but did not find the profession as attractive as he had anticipated. In the meantime his parents, feeling their advancing years, had proposed to him that he come back and locate in another house on the farm. They would retire in a few years and then the property should all be his. Will decided to do so and he and Thelma then moved onto the farm. Her sickness began shortly after that.

Among many irrelevancies, the following facts came to light as Thelma poured out her problems: She had recently fallen in love with another man, married, several years her senior. They had confessed their mutual affection for each other, but had agreed that it was not proper for them to harbor such feelings, and had decided to see no more of each other. But since that her sufferings had increased. It appeared that his appeal to her was in part through their mutual interest in music; she had considerable talent and ambition as a singer and he was a choir leader. Thelma declared she no longer loved her husband, though she formerly did love him dearly, and she knew that he continued still to be deeply in love with her. Their sex life in earlier times had been mutually satisfactory, but she now refused to have marital relations with him, the whole relationship having become loathsome to her. All her husband's efforts at affectionate expression are now repulsive to her. This breach in her affections toward him, however, is not to be attributed to her feelings toward the choir leader, for the reason that they ante-dated this affair and so could not be a result of it.

Thelma's condition was tensely nervous, manifestly psychoneurotic. She insisted that her position had become intolerable and she longed to die. She had several times seriously considered suicide, but her religious convictions had kept her from it, just as they had kept her from eloping with the other man. However, she insisted that she must leave her husband, otherwise she feared she would eventually end her life. She had prayed much over the whole situation but with no relief.

Further inquiry disclosed the fact that she loathed farm life, and had so told her husband before their marriage. He was then looking forward to a medical career and readily said he had no intention of taking her onto a farm, which was true at that time. Apparently he had not taken the matter with any seriousness. Probably he had forgotten it entirely. So, when his parents later asked him to take over the properties and live in the country, he agreed, with no thought of the former promise to Thelma. As a son he had been in the habit of following their counsel and he did so now, presumably with little consultation with

Thelma. Now that they were on the farm, his parents were always kind and gracious, but they always dominated the situation, Will following their lead, as he had always done in childhood. There was no overt conflict in the family. Will and his parents treating Thelma in her sickness with every consideration. But to Thelma even this had become distressing. To her the whole situation was no longer bearable.

The Sunday afternoon interview lasted more than an hour. As it proceeded, Thelma gradually became more composed. Alison seemed so understanding, and sympathetic, and yet not in a way that indicated he was agreeing with her in her interpretations and purposes. But he and his wife were both calmly confident, as though they felt assured the problem was one which could in some way be worked out satisfactorily. Thelma found herself catching composure from them, as though by some kind of mystic contagion.

Alison was constantly master of the situation. Thelma was doing nearly all the talking, but he was directing it, she following his leads. He was non-committal to her, partly because it was best at this time, partly because he was as yet non-committal to himself. This was to be his first diagnosis in his new enterprise, and he would not proceed hurriedly. Fortunately Thelma decided to remain with them several days, which would give him time to think things through and to have further interviews. Graciously and with quiet understanding, he drew from her further information, particularly such as threw additional light on her emotional experiences, in many of which there had been subconscious processes of which she was not aware but which, he surmised, had much to do with the hysteria which had emerged, and would probably account for the rise of her later infatuation for another man. He then told her that he wanted to think the whole matter over and talk further with her later. In the meantime she was to enjoy herself with Mrs. Alison and he was confident some satisfactory solution would be found for her problems. Thelma had become quiet and quite evidently had confidence in him. He saw this and knew that healing had already begun.

That night and for a couple of days, Alison carefully analyzed what he had learned from Thelma. A few more short interviews brought out additional information that he felt was needed. Then he formulated his conclusions:

Thelma, he decided, was suffering from the results of an emotional shock produced by Will's ignoring entirely his promise not to take her to live on the farm, and proceeding to do so under the counsel of his parents, with no evident concern over what it might mean to Thelma. This shock had been far more devastating than Thelma herself realized. It was not merely the wrecking of her dreams of being the wife of a physician, not merely the going to the disliked farm life, not merely the thwarting of other ambitions connected with the situations into which she had expected her life with Will would lead. It was something far deeper, something that cut into the most sensitive fibres of her soul. Will, whom she had thought to be the embodiment of honor and devoted to her with an affection above all others, had tossed both lightly aside and deferred to the desire of his parents. She, who, as an only child, had always been considered, found her interests and preferences apparently taken so lightly that they were not even considered in this decision. Still more, this indicated that his devotion to his parents and deferences to their desires still held first place in his life, or at least so much so that he could forget a promise to her which she considered sacred. It was this shocking disappointment which cut into her soul.

She had said nothing about it. It would have been far better if she had done so. Then Will in all likelihood would have come to realize, as he in all likelihood was not yet doing, that his inconsiderateness had deeply hurt her. In all probability he would have tried at once to make amends. That in itself would have helped, for it would have shown that he did esteem her interests more highly than his hasty actions had indicated. At the very least, her emotions would have found expression if she had talked about it. But she said nothing. More than that, she did not even formulate the meaning of all this in her own mind. On the other hand, she buried the whole emotional experience deep in the recesses of her unconscious mind, where it festered into a complex which broke out in the hysteria from which emerged her various ills. Medical aid as such was, of course, of no avail, because the real source of her ailments was in her soul, beyond the reach of either medicine or scalpel.

And that had not been all. Her complex was not content with physical expression in sickness. It broke out also in a revulsion of feeling toward her husband, and in loathing of the love relations she formerly enjoyed. It went still further and demanded erotic expression with another man. But this was something which her religious convictions would not countenance, and that threw her back into further emotional tensions. From all of this she could now see no escape, not even death, which she had come to desire as release from her present entanglements, because her religious convictions would not allow her to seek it. This bleeding wound in her soul was the source of her other troubles. Until it was healed, nothing else could avail.

His diagnosis outlined, Alison was now ready to begin treatment. First of all there must be the interpretation to Thelma herself. Without dwelling unduly at this time on her physical ills, she was to be told substantially what had been determined in the diagnosis. The interpretation would enable her to understand the ambivalence of her feelings toward her husband; how she now both loves and hates him. The shock brought about this ambivalence. But at the same time she cannot find satisfaction in love for another. The ambivalence prevents that also. To have eloped with another man for whom she had developed an infatuation, would only have increased her emotional confusion. For she was not really in love with the other man; her ambivalent subconsciousness was using him both to punish Will and to afford a compensation to the satisfaction of her own hurt ego.

Furthermore, to have eloped thus would have violated her religious loyalties to her moral ideals, thus making for still further emotional confusion. Also, she knows that Will still loves her, and would be heart-broken if she were thus to leave him. That would always be a source of sorrow. She had therefore done wisely in breaking with the other man. Whatever the way out of her troubles, it certainly was not with him. Her physical ills were largely the result of her mental anxieties which had broken down her resistance. If only they could be relieved, she would probably be able to recover health by nature's own processes.

Little more could be done for her at the start. She must be encouraged to wait for further developments. Her religious faith and understanding can help in that. "Wait, I say, on the Lord" is a counsel of the psalmist which should give her guidance and comfort in the present situation. Musing over these interpretations would help clarify her understanding of herself as well as of her situation. Her resentment of what Will had done was also to be faced by her as something which had been perfectly natural on her part. However, now that she understands the situation somewhat differently, his actions do not seem quite so harsh. She must realize that Will does have obligations to his parents also, which it was perfectly natural and really commendable in him to try to meet, and all the indications are that both Will and his parents are even yet entirely ignorant of her emotional distresses which lay back of her other troubles. What the solution of her problems would be no one could yet say. She could rest assured, however, that her physical ailments and other troubles would adjust themselves when the disturbances in her soul were relieved. While that was being worked out, her Christian faith should enable her to say,

> "So long thy hand hath led me, sure it still
> Will lead me on!"

Alison's next task was to get into touch with Will. It was highly desirable that this be done without either the participation or knowledge of Thelma. Then would come the task of a similar interpretation to Will, whose whole character and background were of a kind that indicated he would be ardent to make amends, even though he might find it difficult to understand. It would take some skill to impress him with the gravity of the situation and to bring him to realize that the fault was primarily his own. But once this was done, and with a manifest understanding that it was an unintentional injury on his part, the sorrow he was sure to feel over his thoughtlessness having caused Thelma so much suffering could be counted on to express itself so honestly that she would believe and understand. When that should come about, the cure would be at hand. With the intelligence and Christian ideals they both possessed, details of adjustment could safely be left to work themselves out one by one.

But why should a situation of this kind be the concern of a minister?

Because religion is so manifestly mixed up in the whole etiology of the case. No psychiatrist who did not have an understanding appreciation of the functioning of the religious motif in the lives of all the persons involved, could possibly have secured the rapport necessary to work out an adjustment. On the other hand, a religious leader was precisely the one to whom they would most readily turn. And his understanding guidance and stimulation of their religious endeavor and response throughout the process would itself be a therapeutic factor of the first value. The sickness was primarily a sickness of the soul.

Alison's first case showed the need of the very kind of service he had set himself to provide.

The Beanings

A few days after the Sunday episode when Thelma disclosed her troubles, Alison was approached with another case which greatly surprised him. A leading man in his church came to him to tell of marital troubles of long standing, and of which no one else seems to have had any suspicion. It took months of work and tested the best skill Alison was able to muster both on his own part and that of others whose help was enlisted. But the ultimate outcome was rich in gratifying results. The story can only be told as a whole and thus necessarily overlaps other features in this narrative.

The Beanings had been married twelve years. Both had grown up in Second Church and were widely known in the community. He was a leading insurance broker and owner of considerable property. She had been a school teacher before her marriage and still continued as a teacher in the nearby high school. Mrs. Beaning and her mother, who lived with them, owned the house in which the family resided; also considerable other property. All were active members of Second Church; Mrs. Beaning was the organist and Mr. Beaning a member of the official board. There were no children.

Mrs. Beaning had been an only child. Her father died when she was fifteen, after which time she and her mother lived together in close fellowship. At the time of their marriage Beaning wanted his wife to go with him to set up a home of their own, but Mrs. Beaning's mother insisted they should live with her and that was done. Beaning wanted his wife to stop teaching, but her mother objected and she continued to teach. Her salary went with her mother's income into a budget separate from her husband's accounts, he paying a weekly stipend into their fund. Mr. and Mrs. Beaning each had an automobile.

When Beaning came to his pastor for counsel, he revealed the fact that he and his wife desired to separate. They had considered doing so for a long time but had held back because of fear that ensuing publicity would embarrass their business affairs and their standing in the community. They were not unmindful also of what it would mean to the church for which they both had a real affection. Beaning himself had high esteem for his wife and a real affection for her. But he felt that he was entirely outside her life, "a mere boarder in the house," as he phrased it. Inquiry brought out the fact that they occupied separate bedrooms and that marital intimacy had not occurred a dozen times in their married life. She was frigid and uninterested. However, she esteemed her husband and had no antipathies toward him. To outward appearances there was nothing amiss with their marriage. But in reality it was without content. Beaning felt that things had reached a stage where he could no longer endure his unnatural position.

It was a real shock to Alison when Beaning came asking for a conference and uncovered his problem. Of all people, Alison felt these were just about the last whom he would have thought likely to come with a problem like this. Everybody in the church had assumed the Beanings were beautifully adjusted and finding life together most worth while. If this situation obtained with them, how about others? Here was one more evidence that Alison was going to find his case work cut out for him, at least at present, right among his own people. Once again it seemed, charity was to begin at home.

And yet, now that the matter had come out, Alison remembered that Beaning had often showed a restiveness he could not quite understand. His laugh, too, in group merriment, sometimes seemed forced, and Alison had caught himself wondering what it might mean. But he had always dismissed the matter as of no consequence. Now it did have meaning.

How many such cases may this church contain?

"And if they do these things in a green tree, what shall be done in a dry?"

The two men talked together in utter frankness. More and more, in response to Alison's understanding questions, Beaning revealed the yearnings of his hungry heart. It was not that he was particularly concerned about physical sex relations; that in itself was evidently not much in his thought. But it was the utter outsideness he felt from his wife's real affections and life interests. Nowhere was he finding between them that interflow of soul with soul which he had expected marriage to afford and for which his heart was yearning with a feeling that it was something to which one is entitled, something God made human hearts to enjoy. Not once did he express resentment, not once did he chide. The one thing manifest was a lonesome, hungry heart.

Alison closed the interview telling Beaning frankly he did not know now what to advise him to do; he would have to study the situation carefully, then he would talk with Beaning again. In the meantime, he must not become discouraged. After all, both he and his wife were Christian at heart, sincerely wanting to do whatever would be most helpful to all concerned. Because we are Christians, we believe that when we trust God and do our best, we will find a way.

To Alison this case was of the greatest concern. He esteemed both Beaning and his wife highly and was most solicitous that he should not make any mistake. So he went to another man whose wider experience he felt assured would be of help to him. Together they went over all the facts available, worked out their diagnosis and outlined a program.

To start with, they agreed that this was a clear case of mother fixation on the part of Mrs. Beaning. When her father died, she being in her middle teen age, the bereaved mother made a transfer of her affectional expression to the daughter, onto whom she now proceeded to pour all the love formerly directed toward the father. The daughter was just then at that perilous age in her emotional development when she should have been emerging from the normal homoerotic stage of the young girl whose love is primarily for her own sex, particularly for her mother, into the hetero-erotic stage of emerging womanhood, when her interests should reach out toward those of the opposite sex. Normally the earlier years of this interest in the opposite sex are ones in which it is polygamous, or rather, with a girl, polyandrous, years in which she is interested in all the boys but does not want to be tied down to any particular one. Later this attitude changes and the urge becomes monogamous, she falls in love with some one person, presumably for life. But during the earlier stage of no settled affection for any one male, it is relatively easy for a girl to be thrown back to the earlier stage of homoerotic love for one of her own sex. Precisely this is what had happened to Mrs. Beaning. In response to her mother's out-pouring of her entire affectional life upon her, she had literally fallen in love with her mother and they have been in love with each other ever since.

When, in the course of time, she grew older and was courted by Beaning, it seemed, of course, to be the proper thing for her to marry him. That sort of thing is the conventional one for all nice girls to do, and Beaning was in every way an acceptable husband. But fall in love with him she could not. She was already fully attached in those emotional regards to her mother, and her mother had no intention whatever of surrendering what she herself so much enjoyed. Mrs. Beaning was in such a state that she could not even realize that there was any other kind of emotional relation possible toward a man than the respect in which she held the one she agreed to marry. The regression into which she had been thrown by her mother precluded any experience of even natural yearnings for emotional responses from the other sex. By insisting on continuing to live with them, the mother had seen to it that there would be no release of the girl's affections from a first attachment to herself. The downright selfishness of the mother in this was something of which she was herself entirely unconscious. But that did not prevent its devastating effects upon the daughter. Her sex frigidity toward her husband inevitably followed. For a woman's sex life, unlike that of a man, has to be awakened, and this is normally brought about by the efforts for expression of an emotional attachment such as Mrs. Beaning had never been able to experience toward her husband because of her mother fixation.

It was quite evident, therefore, that the unwholesome relationships in the Beaning marriage, were the results, the inescapable results of the conditionings to which Mrs. Beaning had been subjected. It was impossible for her to react otherwise. Beaning was indeed nothing more than "a boarder in the house," for the reason that she felt the need of nothing more. Indeed, there was no particular need of even this in her life, aside from the conventional custom of being married, for she and her mother were financially independent and had practically all their major interests in common with each other, with Beaning on the outside.

As Alison and his counselor discussed the case together, they decided that any adjustment would necessarily begin with devolping a sense of certain needs on the part of Mrs. Beaning. There were three aspects of her life in relation to which this might be undertaken, three changes which might make her feel the need of a husband: She might become financially dependent upon him; she might, by separation from her mother, be brought to experience an emotional need for response which would suggest him as a possible source of satisfaction; finally, she might be brought to realize that a woman's sex nature endowed her with possibilities of gratifying experiences which she had never known but which other women enjoyed. They decided efforts should be made along all three of these lines.

Just how the start on the first of these was effected has never been explained, but shortly after this Mrs. Beaning was notified by the school authorities that she would not be re-employed for the coming school year. It was suggested as a reason that there were younger women in the community amply able to do the same teaching and it was only fair that one of them be given an opportunity, particularly since Mrs. Beaning had no special financial need of it. Thus she found her financial independence much abridged. Her mother let her know it was not exactly to her liking to have to support the daughter. It was really quite gratifying, therefore, that she had a husband able and ready to support her as his wife.

Shortly after that her mother's health became impaired and she spent a short time in the hospital. While she was there, suggestions came from various sources that it would be good for her health if she were to spend the winter with her sister in Florida. Her physician, Dr. Rogers, strongly supported the proposal, no doubt following some suggestive hints from Alison, who was really responsible for others making similar recommendations to her. So arrangements were made for her to spend six months in the sunny South. That left Mrs. Beaning for the first time in her life without the companionship and emotional response of her mother. Life for her now came to have something of loneliness. She found herself reaching out for some one to love. Of course, there was Beaning.

Thus it came about in a relatively short time that approaches had been made along two of the possible lines which Alison and his counselor had selected for constructive efforts to awaken normal emotional desires on the part of Mrs. Beaning toward her husband. Alison never said what part he had taken in bringing these two series of events about, but he did insist that God had a lot to do with it. He was of profound conviction that there is a "Divinity that shapes our ends," a providence that figures in the world processes about us, and when we maintain a prayerful attitude of response to God's leadings, all things will work together for good and often in ways beyond our comprehending.

The time now seemed ripe for effort along the third line also. Here Alison's tactful wife was brought into the picture. Without explaining to her more than was needful, she was told of the strained relations between the Beanings, and of the fact that lack of sex response between them was an important factor in the situation. Mrs. Beaning's frigidity was also interpreted to her, and she was told of the indications that it had its seat in nothing organic, but purely in the woman's ignorance and lack of normal maturity in those relations.

Shortly after that, Mrs. Alison managed to get into a conversation with another young married woman in the presence of Mrs. Beaning, in which the two of them talked frankly about the fact that the establishment of understanding sex relations make so much for mutual appreciation between husband and wife. The conversation was purely casual and in apparent assumption that Mrs. Beaning was in full accord, from her own experience, with what was being said. The other young woman, of course, knew nothing of Mrs. Alison's purpose in the conversation. A few days later practically the same thing occurred with another married woman, again in the presence of Mrs. Beaning, Mrs. Alison doing most of the talking and directing the conversation.

The natural result followed. Mrs. Beaning came to Mrs. Alison to learn more about the subject.

Her curiosity was aroused. More than that, she had come to realize there was something in the experiences of those other women which she had never known and which seemed to have been highly valued by them as an appreciated bond in the marital relation. Still more, she was burdened with the distressing consciousness that her own marriage was going on the rocks. Well she knew that her own relations with her husband had been very different. Did that, perhaps, figure in their failure to sustain mutual appreciation and fellowship?

She frankly acknowledged to Mrs. Alison that she had been interested in the remarks she had heard, because of her own lack of both knowledge and experience in the fields about which they had been talking. Of course, she said nothing about her own strained relations with Mr. Beaning of which she supposed Mrs. Alison knew nothing.

Mrs. Alison then proceeded tactfully on the sex education of Mrs. Beaning, doing it in a way that relieved embarrassment, aroused still further interest and kindled confidence that she too might attain what the other women had experienced. Mrs. Beaning listened with intense interest, but just as evident bewilderment. Had this counsel come from almost anyone else than her pastor's wife, whom she so much trusted and esteemed, she would have felt impelled to dismiss it as immoral or at least immodest and unfitting for any cultured woman. Had she not always been given to understand by her mother and others that all sex talk was degrading, that nice people, particularly nice women never thought about such things? Had not all her Christian teaching been to put away the things of the flesh? She found all her previous ideals of womanhood rising in rebellion against the suggestions coming from these conversations.

And yet? No, they would not down that easily. Ever since she overheard that first conversation she could not put away these suggestions from her mind, much as she tried to do so. Always there was rising up the remembrance that these women were evidently happily married and that her own marriage was rapidly heading toward disaster.

She was torn by terrific conflict. On the one side was her old idealism, fortified by all her intense religious convictions with which her experience and teaching had so closely tied it. On the other was her sense of tragedy in her own shattered romance, her feeling of incompleteness in her marital experience in comparison with what she had recently heard, her admiration for Mrs. Alison and confidence in her as a woman of finest Christian culture and character. Her very soul seemed in the process of being torn asunder.

It was a crisis for Mrs. Beaning greater than she at that time realized. In after years, when she could think it over in calmer retrospect, what it might have meant to her stood out in awful portent. She thanked God that her counselor that day had been a Christian woman who guided her with both an intelligent understanding and a Christian heart. What if she had been in the hands of one to whom religion was not of serious moment? She knew herself well enough to realize that one of two things would have emerged: either she would have decided to seek the satisfactions which gave promise of saving her marriage from ruin and to throw over her ethical resistances, or she would have turned against the suggestions on the basis of her moral ideals and religious convictions. If she had done the former, her religion would have been wrecked; if she had done the latter, her marriage would have been wrecked.

And that was not all. She now had enough additional information to realize that in either case she would have gone into the ensuing years with conflicts buried deep in her soul which would in all likelihood have driven her finally into some kind of a neurosis, probably ruining her health or her character, perhaps both.

Mrs. Alison was not a trained social worker, but she was an intelligent young woman of considerable experience and alert feminine intuition. Underneath the taut features of the woman before her, she perceived there was a raging emotional conflict which the sufferer could neither escape nor understand. Deftly Mrs. Alison lifted the idea of the relations of sex between man and wife to entirely different levels. As she discussed them, they seemed far from merely the satisfaction of biological urges. She discussed them as God-given potencies for expression of the sublimest spiritual appreciations, binding together two souls that love and that seek above all else to be a blessing to each other. For that reason, also, the entering of these most intimate relations in any other way than as the supreme expression of a life-dominating affection, is prostitution of what God designed to be holy. That would be true, even if the parties were married to each other. It would be true of the woman who married only for money or for the security of a home, and it would be true of the man who married to secure a housekeeper. But when there is a deeply welling affection and constantly growing appreciation between two souls that long to give all they have and are to each other in an outflow of soul to soul, then these relations become beautiful and sacred.

With that kind of idealism, Mrs. Beaning felt that her religion could attach itself without restraint. In something like this, she believed, these other women were enjoying lives free from the conflict now tearing at her own soul, lives without the spiritual poverties in their relations with their husbands which she now so clearly saw had through all these years obtained between her and Mr. Beaning, lives enriched by the ties which make a man willingly forsake his father and mother and cleave unto his wife as they twain become one flesh.

"A man shall forsake his father and mother and cleave unto his wife"—did not the Bible set that as an ideal? Then should not the wife do likewise?

Mrs. Beaning's heart was struck with dismay at the thought, with a cutting sense of guilt. "Forsake—mother!" Had she not done the very opposite? Had she not very deliberately allowed herself to cleave unto her own mother? She had always thought of that close fellowship between them as something very beautiful. Now it looked so different. Perhaps, after all, it was largely selfishness on the part of that mother that tried to hold the daughter to her? She had never thought of it in that way before. Those binding ties between them of which she had always been so proud; they now loomed up as anything but beautiful.

And Beaning! Patient, long-suffering Beaning! Through all these years he had allowed himself to be shut out of that intimacy in her whole womanly being which her vows at the altar had promised! Her heart sank with a shocked sense of guilt. Her own marriage wrecked by the cruel selfishness of her mother and herself! And Beaning! What a real man he had shown himself to be by the way he had endured their selfish slightings! With her rising sense of guilt she found herself warming with a new affection for this man whom she had so wickedly wronged these many years. How lonesome his soul must have been!

Of course, not a word of all this which was rushing through the mind of Mrs. Beaning was spoken to her counseling friend. Indeed, she was saying almost nothing. But as they parted Mrs. Alison could see a new light in the eyes of this recently so distracted woman. With a quiet suggestion anent the Christian's confidence with which one prays over such a situation and then awaits the guidance of God through both inner conviction and outer circumstance, she was content to let the leaven work.

When Beaning returned from his office that evening, he seemed to his wife to be a different man. Was he different? No, as she thought again, she decided he probably was just the same as he had been. It was she who could now see things about him to which she had long been blind. When one confronts a great new revelation of one's self to one's self, one seems to live half a lifetime in a day. So it was with Mrs. Beaning. What a flood of new ideas, new emotions, new outlooks had swept over her during these few hours! Mother now away in Florida, Beaning now alone with her in what is after all their home, the home of them twain, yes, things did look different tonight. Beaning seemed different. Her heart was reaching out for him in a strange new way, a way she had never known before.

She was falling in love with her husband.

Beaning on his part was actually only slightly different. He of course, had been given to know nothing of what was being undertaken with his wife. But he had been guided in his own expressions and attitudes toward her. And he had been told that, now her mother was away, it was possible his wife would be drawn toward him more closely. In that case, an appropriate response on his part might further better relations between them. He had been given counsel on helpful procedures on the part of a man toward a wife whose sex potencies may be in the process of awakening, and interpretations which would help forward emerging spiritual appreciations and their physical expression in ways that would be spiritually wholesome. Thanks to the new light in which Alison had enabled him to see his situation, he no longer thought of it as hopeless. And he had enough new understanding of his wife to be able to respond intelligently to any advances on her part.

Long before the return of Mrs. Beaning's mother from her southern trip, a new understanding and appreciation had come to full fruition between the Beanings. For the first time they were deeply in love with each other, and in each other they were finding full satisfaction. All the rich meaning which Mrs. Beaning had heard her women friends attach to their marital relations was now hers. All thought of divorce was now only an amusing memory.

Two years later Alison baptized their first baby. And Mrs. Beaning's mother, who had come back from the South to find the first place in her daughter's heart now given to another, found a new and holy joy in experiencing the affections of a grandmother.

Maxine

A third case which came quickly on the heels of those of Thelma and the Beanings, involved another of the leading families in Second Church.

Maxine was a married woman of forty-five, healthy except for "nervousness" which had come to take the form of frequent outbreaks much akin to the temper tantrums of a child. Her husband was a railroad conductor to whom she had been married at eighteen. There were two children, a daughter twenty-five and a son twenty. Maxine's mother, aged eighty, lived with the family. Maxine was an only child, the father dying when she was sixteen.

All were actively religious people. The grandmother had been an outstanding leader in the organized women's work of the church for years, and was now proudly rounding out her fortieth year as president of the missionary society. Maxine was also active in the church. And her husband was one of the deacons. A bit pessimistic, the people thought him to be, and often with a dejected look which Alison found suggesting that somehow he had come to feel defeated in life. The son was away in college. The daughter was an efficient stenographer and office clerk, holding an important position in the court house. The daughter's income was turned in each month to her mother, Maxine, who purchased all her clothing for her and gave her spending money from time to time as requested.

For something over a year the daughter had been keeping company with a young engineering student in the University, who was now about to complete his work there and who was already under contract for a promising position with a corporation in the Middle West. He had been a regular attendant at Second Church for two years and active in the young peoples work of the church. He seemed to have the full approval of Maxine and her family.

Only a few days after Beaning came to Alison with his problems, this young engineer came to see the minister. Thus Alison found his third case also within his own church family, another case with which he had to wrestle while dealing with those of Thelma and the Beanings.

The young man told of his perplexities as to what should be done concerning difficulties which had arisen in connection with his relations to Maxine's daughter. Nearly a year before, she had told her mother that the young engineer had proposed marriage to her. They felt they were really in love with each other, and she had decided to accept his proposal. That would mean their marriage following his graduation the next Spring, and going to live in the Middle West. Immediately Maxine flew into a rage and opposed the marriage vehemently. The next time the young man appeared she drove him from the house and forbad him ever to speak to her daughter again. She acknowledged that she had nothing in particular against him, that she really admired him. But she insisted her daughter should never marry a man who would take her away from the community in which she lived. After a time the young couple, who were very much in love with each other and who tried to win Maxine to a different attitude, did succeed in getting her permission for the young man to come again to the house, and she even acceded in a self-pitying way to their proposed marriage. But she announced that she would commit suicide the day it occurred. She treated the young man with harsh hostility, and was constantly upbraiding the daughter for what she termed her cruelty in proposing to leave her mother who wanted her near.

From the young man Alison learned much more about the inner history of the family. Maxine's mother had always lived with them. She was a dominating character and determined the policies of the household. Following her own husband's death she had dominated Maxine. After Maxine's marriage, her husband soon found that the way to keep a happy home was for him to let her dominate that also. Otherwise, he would have found himself at odds with Maxine, who would brook nothing else than submission to her mother. Following the birth of the second child, Maxine refused to have further marital relations with her husband, saying that she had decided two children were enough for their family. Shortly after that there was some suspicion of intimacies on his part with another woman. Maxine made it the basis of violent attacks on him. To avoid scandal, he broke off friendship with the woman in question, since which time, it appears, he has lived a celibate life, dominated by Maxine and her mother. Always of a quiet, unassertive type, he now became entirely unresisting. To Maxine's frequent outbreaks of temper he always responded by trying to do whatever she demanded. In the matter of the daughter's proposed marriage, he counseled submission, though he freely stated that he himself fully approved of it.

Under all the circumstances, what should the young man do?

Alison had the young man come back for a second and a third interview before giving advice on the question at issue. He did in the meantime, however, explain to him something of what seemed to be the occasion for Maxine's resistance to the proposed marriage and counseled patience while they tried together to fathom the deeper problems involved. In the meantime he used such other sources as he found available in securing additional light on the situation. In this way he confirmed some things told him by the young man which had been deduced by him and the daughter from things which she did know. Alison was convinced now that these interpretations were correct. Putting all his materials together, Alison formulated his diagnosis.

Here was another case rising out of the tragedy of a mother's misplaced affection. Only, in this case the result was quite different. Here it was one of mother domination and daughter submission under compulsion. Dominated by the mother emotionally, the daughter had never been able to affect a normal emotional transfer to her husband. Such affection as she did experience was still attached to her mother, though too dominated by fear to be satisfying. Presumably because of this there was no normal sex awakening in connection with her marital relations. The refusal to continue such relations after the birth of her two children was a result of this. This lack of affectional response on her part led to her husband seeking at least emotional and perhaps physical satisfaction elsewhere, and discovery of this opened a door for Maxine's libidinal impulses which had never secured a normal outlet, to become diverted into a sadism which flowed out in her tyrannies over her husband and later over her children also. The resistance to her daughter's marrying and moving away, rose out of Maxine's unconscious desire to compensate for her long subservience to her mother by establishing a like relationship for herself over her daughter.

Alison had recently witnessed a moving picture which now seemed to him to throw light upon, or at least to illustrate this case. It was a narrative of a household in which the father in the family group at the dinner table went into a tirade of abuse of his wife and dashed out of the room. Then immediately his wife, who had submitted most meekly to his tirade, turned viciously on her daughter with similar abuse and likewise bolted out of the room. Then the daughter, who had been most abject under her mother's attack, turned in like manner on her little brother, who likewise submitted till she also rushed out of the room, when he, in turn, vented his feelings in abuse of the dog. When he also had gone away the dog solemnly walked across the room to where the family cat was asleep before the fire and kicked the cat!

This same psychology, thought Alison explained in part Maxine's recent conduct. Ever since her daughter's birth, Maxine in her subconscious mind had cherished the expectation that some time this opportunity for compensation would come. But now, when the daughter proposed a marriage that would take her entirely away from the easy contact Maxine had expected to maintain, she saw the complete collapse of all upon which she had pinned her hopes, and for which she had endured the tyrannies of her own mother. The threat of suicide was also natural. It afforded the strongest kind of restraint for the daughter. Moreover, if the daughter were really to go away as proposed, and all her hopes were thus shattered, life would no longer seem worth living.

In the way of prognosis, the outlook for a change for the better on the part of any of the three elders Alison felt to be unlikely. They were too firmly fixed in their present channels. If the daughter were to submit and remain at home, Maxine's tyrannies would constantly increase. If she were to marry, now that the grandmother was getting old, Maxine would shortly be left in the company of her husband only, since the son was already at college and was not expected to return home to live, and that husband, because of his long abject submission to her, she had come to despise. Here was a further cause for the intensity of her resentment. There was, however, no likelihood of her committing suicide. People who threaten to commit suicide seldom do. Should suicide ever occur in her case, it would not be as a reaction against her daughter's marriage, but from a psychosis into which her mental conflicts might sometime throw her.

Alison now felt that the time had come to give some positive counsel. He explained to the young man that Maxine had never been able to think of her daughter in terms other than as a little girl, and that the domination over her rose out of this. When the young man suggested that the daughter was now old enough to assert her own independence, particularly since she was financially self-supporting, Alison advised that efforts along this line should be made gently though they might well be firmly taken. For instance, in the matter of clothing, it might be all right for the girl to proceed to buy some things she desired without consulting her mother, and when the mother protested, very courteously let her know that she now felt herself woman enough to make such decisions for herself. Alison felt that it would be wise for the girl to begin now to assert her self-determination in relatively small things. That would prepare the mother for what would later be a more serious proposal.

For a few weeks the daughter proceeded along the lines to which Alison had agreed, gradually taking over control of more and more of her own life. Maxine responded by assuming a self-pitying attitude, complaining that the daughter no longer respected her as she should, but the daughter said nothing in return. One evening the two of them went for a walk together. Maxine again brought up the proposed marriage and demanded that it be given up. This the daughter told her firmly would not be done. She went on to say that she felt her mother had no right to make such a demand, since she had no personal objections to the young man himself. Maxine must understand this decision was final. The next day Maxine, instead of committing suicide, left home, saying she would not return as long as the daughter remained there. A second and third day she remained away, the father constantly becoming more alarmed.

Then without consulting Alison, the young woman

took things into her own hands. Sending one morning for her lover she said, "Do you really want to marry me?" On receiving his affirmative reply she said, "Then you are going to do it today!" Still not consulting Alison, they went to a minister who was a friend of the young man in an adjoining state and were married. Returning to her office later in the day, she telephoned to her father telling him what had been done. That night she spent with a girl friend.

The next morning she received a scurrilous letter from her mother enclosing a copy of another letter which the mother said she was sending to the prospective employers of the young man. In this she accused him of having seduced her daughter. She also instructed her daughter to come and take away her personal belongings immediately or they would be burned. Then she would commit suicide and the daughter would forever be guilty of her death!

At this point the young people again came to Alison. The father was distracted and pleading with them, and they were in the natural reaction from their splurge of independence and uncertain what to do. Alison would not have counseled such a course as they had taken, but he was secretly rather glad they had done it. Without passing judgment on that, he explained that their question now was what to do next. They need not fear suicide. Maxine's recent conduct showed clearly that this was only a threat. But there was something else they should do. Together they then composed a letter which the young woman sent by messenger to her mother:

My Dear Mother:—

I have just received your letter, together with the enclosed copy of one you say you are sending to John's prospective employers. I am very sorry you feel as you do about our marriage. But you and I have already talked enough about that. However, I hope you realize the seriousness of this charge you have made against John in the letter to his employers. The charges are untrue, as you well know. But in writing them you have been guilty of criminal libel for which John could now have you arrested and perhaps sent to prison. I am very sorry you did this. We will come this afternoon and secure my things.

In spite of your feelings toward me for which I am truly sorry, I still subscribe myself,

Your loving daughter,

Lucile.

That afternoon the young people drove out to the home to secure the young woman's belongings. Maxine met them at the door, threw herself into her daughter's arms, and with many tears asked them both to forgive her. Instead of taking away the young woman's things, they spent the night in the home.

Neither Maxine nor any of the rest of the family ever came to know that Alison had anything to do with the matter. The young people went to the West shortly after that. A year later the grandmother died. For the young people, the solution has been good. Maxine and her husband have continued to approve of them and what they are doing.

But for Maxine herself and her husband, no adjustment has yet been found. Maxine continues to be subject to her tantrums, tyrannous over her husband, more furiously so at times now that her mother is dead. He in turn seems to grow more beaten and glum than ever. Alison has not found a solution. Manifestly, after so many years of abnormal emotional relations between them as man and wife and with both of them now quite mature in years, it is practically impossible to re-channel their natural urges along normal lines of expression. Alison is working at sublimation into religious work, in which both are interested. With the husband he seems to be making considerable headway. Like blind Matheson, whose fiancee had forsaken him when he was suddenly stricken blind and who turned to God with what he expressed in his familiar verses, "Oh Love that will not let me go!" so this man seems to be finding in God an object for his love that is likewise satisfying. But Maxine thus far fails to respond. She remains querulous, frequently distracted, always unhappy, her only satisfactions, apparently, in her miseries. Alison wonders whether she is already a lost soul. But he cannot bring himself to despair. He is still working for her redemption.

Of one thing he is certain: the only hope for her is religion. A psychiatrist with whom he has taken up the case fully, considers it incurable. The channeling of her basic urges into these forms of sadistic expression he declares to be now too firmly set. It is to be remembered also that she is securing whatever satisfactions she does enjoy in life from precisely these sources. To give them up would be to surrender the very things whereby she now demonstrates to herself some evidences of her superiority. It is only in regard to her religious idealism and loyalties that she finds herself in conscious conflict. Formerly she had been able to meet this by an ascetic conception of Christian morals, by assuming that there is virtue in the mere crushing of natural impulse and that there is something sanctifying in such suffering. Her mother had schooled her in that type of perverted puritanism. As a girl, Maxine had sometimes wondered whether anything one enjoys must for that reason be suspect. Nevertheless, she had built her patterns of life around those teachings. In these later years, however, she has been hearing a very different kind of Christian teaching, one emphasizing wholesome self expression and the direction or sublimation of every impulse, sex included, into some helpful outflow. Maxine found this throwing her into terrific conflict. For a time she fought the new teachings bitterly. She undertook to organize a committee against birth control and against the teaching of sex hygiene to youth. But she found the tides of Christian thinking against her. At the same time the moral shipwrecks she had so freely predicted would result from the new teaching failed to appear. To appearances of defeat she responded with increased tantrums, but these only left her exhausted and commonly with feelings of frustation against which she was powerless.

Alison is watching all of this carefully. In his sermons he frequently emphasizes the regenerating power of the Holy Spirit when given free way to surge through the whole of one's being including the deeper unconscious processes and to sanctify the expression of every urge into what makes for loving helpfulness and thereby for peace and joy in living. Maxine listens and grows more restless. The conflict is without doubt taking more definite form and increasing. Alison is watching and praying that one of these days it will develop into a more open warfare in her soul which she may more clearly see and understand, and that she will then break through into a divinely regenerated life. It is her only hope.

IV

BEYOND FREUD

ALISON followed a policy of avoiding all unnecessary publicity. It had been necessary to take his own people fully into confidence concerning the program, but beyond that he realized publicity would be much more of an injury than a help.

But such things cannot be confined to the corner in which they are done, when people are being benefited because they are well done. The world will make a path to the door of him who produces the better mouse trap. For the same reason outside interest sprang up over what was being accomplished in Second Church. Reporters and feature writers sought out Alison for a "story," but he turned them graciously away. He knew that publicity would embarrass his work, both by keeping away timid people whom he could help and by attracting certain more or less psychopathic types of cranks and faddists for whom he could do little or nothing. He was determined not to sacrifice the good he could do by the self-advertising which might feed one's vanity and inflate his ego, or even invite an opportunity for another field with greater emoluments. He even refused invitations to make speeches about it in religious gatherings till he had been following his program some years. He saw his task as doing things helpful rather than talking about it.

The one exception he made was in being willing always to talk personally with another minister, or person in other work who came for counsel regarding similar efforts in which they were engaged or which they wished to project. With such he was always ready to share the best from his own experience. He did this the more readily because he realized that most ministers had not enjoyed the background of clinical training he had received in other connections and was now using here. For that very reason he knew the dangers that beset them. Without realizing how utterly unfit they were for the more intricate work in situations where there is need of delicate skill, perhaps that of a psychiatrist or other specialist, they are likely to rush in with snap judgments and do far more harm than good. But he found that in many cases he was able to suggest ways in which they could do yeoman services with life situations of kinds for which they could easily equip themselves to deal.

Nearly two years after the new program was started he received a visit from Phil Perkins, a former classmate in the seminary, who had written asking for an extended conference. He had been reading widely on the subject, had started in a small way in his own parish, and had gone far enough it seemed, to realize how little he knew about it. Alison had entertained him at dinner, and they were settled in Alison's library for an evening's chat.

"First thing I want to ask you, Mortimer, is about sex. Are you Freudian?"

"Not particularly. But Freud made most valuable

contributions which all of us, laymen as well as psychiatrists appreciate and can use. Personally, I am not finding sex offenses figuring in most of the cases with which I am dealing. But sex does figure in them, often quite prominently. Let me give you some examples." Then, recounting the three cases of Thelma, the Beanings and Maxine, Alison showed how sex figured largely in all of them, yet in none was there a sex offense, with the possible exception of Maxine's husband, and in that case it was well down the line in the story and incidental to the real problem. All were akin in that the ultimate causes inhered in childhood and adolescent experiences which predisposed the three women to the unfortunate developments that came later in their lives. In both the cases of Mrs. Beaning and Maxine there was a regression to a pre-adolescent form of sex expression in the way of a primary affection for one of their own sex, and in both cases it was brought about by a distorted sense of duty to a mother who herself did not realize that it was just her own selfishness which led her to bind her daughter to herself. In neither of these cases was there a sex offense of the kind condemned by society, but in both there was a sex offense by the mothers which was even more tragic.

"I often recall," he added, "an aphorism I picked up years ago when I was a student. My professor said, 'You will find in your analytic work, that the ultimate source of a sex offense is rarely the sex impulse, and the unwholesome outbreaking of the sex impulse is usually in something other than a sex offense.' The more experience I have, the more I realize that is true."

"For instance?" asked the visitor.

"Mostly sadism and masochism," replied Alison. "Take sadism. My, how common it is! Right here among the best people and in the church! You know very well what is the driving urge back of most of the chatter of the ordinary gossip. Of course, she does not herself know it. With glee her assumed shock poorly conceals, she revels with her friends over the latest morsel of scandal about some girl's alleged sex irregularities, but she would be shocked beyond words if she learned that the psychiatrist sees back of it all, her own repressed sex impulse which has thus found a perverted expression in hurting another. Or take such cases as Maxine's bludgeoned husband. That was pure sadism on her part. You can think of all sort of cruelties among the people you know which are nothing else than sadistic releases for their repressed impulses of sex. Men as well as women are sadists, you know that. A lot of cruelty in business and sport is just sadism.

"Then take masochism, that other perversion of repressed sex in which the sufferer enjoys being made to suffer. Maxine is an example of that also. How delicious she found her self-pity! Or take psychopathic lying and stealing, hysterias of all sorts, neuroses of many kinds now easily uncovered by the psychiatrists, here they are in such numbers and such bewildering confusion, sadisms and masochism all mixed up together among everyday folks as well as the mentally sick with whom the psychiatrists deal. The only fitting name I can think of for this demon of repressed sex is that given by the demoniac Jesus healed at Gadara: 'My name is Legion!'

"Now, take the other side of it. I have for several years been the ministerial consultant at an institution here for young wayward girls, and in that connection I have consulted with and about a large number of them who had records of sex delinquencies. We found that it was rarely the case that there was any evidence of a strong sex urge or even response on the part of these girls. Generally we found the cause in a desire to escape from something, perhaps at home, or to compensate, or to secure attention and seeming appreciation."

"But how about the men?"

"A lot of the same thing there. I was much impressed years ago with what Whiting Williams said about this in his study of 'what is on the worker's mind' based on his experiences as a day laborer in steel mills and elsewhere. Williams said that while stories of sex conquests were commonly being told among the men, he was convinced that some of it was mere braggadocio, and most of the exploits that had been undertaken were largely compensations for the conditions of their toil. Men driven and ordered and bossed, go seeking conquest to satisfy themselves that they, too, can subdue others. Men with nerves draggled by monotonous tasks go seeking thrills, something exciting, and sex seems promising. My own observation convinces me he is right.

"Personally, I find I am more and more making

what might be called an Adlerian approach. That is, I seem to find the key to most of the cases in my work in a longing for self-realization, seeking escape from feeling inferior. You can take it for granted that every person wants to feel that he is worthwhile in the world, that he really is some pebble on the beach. Every Jack Horner who has to sit in a corner, wants some time to put in his thumb and pull out a plum, so that he can say, 'What a great boy am I!' He'll even risk his life to do it."

"Then you don't believe that saying in the Bible: 'All that a man hath will he give for his life'?"

"I do not. Anyhow, it was the devil that said it. But all a man hath will he give for his self respect. I always keep that in mind when I am trying to help people out of their troubles. The worse fix he is in, the worse features he has shown of himself, so much the more must I find something in him which he himself can be made to believe can be so brought out as to make him worthwhile."

"How about what others think of him?"

"That's about next in importance. And it is very important in most cases. Shakespeare was right, when a man has lost his reputation and feels he has done so, he does feel that he has 'lost the immortal part' of himself, and 'all the rest is bestial!' "

"That interests me," said Perkins. "It interests me a lot. I am thinking of it just now in connection with a case in my own field that is distressing me. This may give me my clue. I'd like to tell you about it. Indeed, that's one reason for my coming."

"Go ahead," replied Alison.

The two men then started to confer together on a case on which they were to work together for nearly two years and then end in disappointment. Alison could never think of it afterwards without regret and somewhat of resentment. It ended tragically, the problem unsolved. Alison cannot get away from the conviction that this woman went to an untimely grave because of the narrow ignorant prejudice of a physician more jealous for his professional prerogatives than concerned for the welfare of the suffering woman. In response to Alison's invitation, Perkins laid the case before him as it then stood.

Katherine Brightman

I first met Mrs. Brightman a year ago last July. Her husband is a regular attendant at my church. I had been told she was an invalid. Shortly after I met her, she asked me to take her with me to a district young peoples meeting, saying she thought she would enjoy the ride. As we visited on the way, I observed that she seemed to be very nervous, apparently with a feeling of inferiority of some kind. She could not look me in the eye. At the meeting where I was one of the speakers, she seemed to drink in everything I was saying. Months later she repeated to me things I had said which I myself had forgotten. She avows that she that day began to get back her faith in human nature. She attended the church service the following Sunday, the first time in several years. After that she did not miss a Sunday till January, when she became ill. She has not been out of the house since that time. The doctor has diagnosed the case as tuberculosis.

Mrs. Brightman is a woman in her early forties. Her husband is a farmer, quiet, hard-working, kindly. The family is quite poor. He is very devoted to his wife, and she often speaks appreciatively of the many nice things he does for her. His mother, who is very old, lives with them as did his father till his death about a year ago. There is a daughter eighteen years old. The family relations seem entirely harmonious. There are, however, a number of in-laws on his side, who apparently look with disfavor and with some kind of suspicion on Katherine.

From what I can learn, the earlier years of Katherine's marriage were not so happy. They lived here in the city, where her husband was employed rather long hours in a factory. Katherine seems to have lived at that time a somewhat gay life, and went out a great deal to social affairs without her husband, who had little interest in them. A little later they moved to their present home on the farm with his father. This life proved quite dull for Katherine, and she took frequent trips to see her city friends. After a time a son was born to whom they were both much devoted. When he was eight years old he met with an accident which caused his death. Mrs. Brightman was crushed and soon became bitter, accusing God of taking her son away from her. When, a few years later, a daughter was born she relaxed somewhat in her bitterness, feeling, she says, that God was again friendly to her.

She has few friends, most people now looking on her as "somewhat queer." I observed that there was one person in whom she seemed particularly interested, a Portuguese girl who keeps house for an unmarried man, and about whom there has been some gossip. Mrs. Brightman thinks the girl is being "persecuted," and mentions it in a way that makes me think she in some way identifies the girl with herself.

I have suspected that Mrs. Brightman's illness was at least in part and perhaps primarily mental, so I have been trying to cultivate her confidence, in the hope that she would uncover anything that might be troubling her. At first she was quite reserved, though showing quite definitely that she respected and trusted me. At times she would begin to talk quite freely, then break off, perhaps in the middle of a sentence, and begin talking about something else entirely unrelated. Soon she began writing me letters. These were disconnected, as was her conversation. In both she would frequently tell me there was something she wanted to tell me but just couldn't. Frequently she would apparently be on the point of doing so, then would break off suddenly. It was evident that her courage failed her. I once suggested to her that she join the church. She seemed quite overcome that I should ask her; said she felt so unworthy. She still refuses to do so, although she declares that our conferences have been bringing her real joys in religious experience. But she still refers to her "unworthiness."

The two men went over the facts as Perkins had narrated them with great care. It was evident there was some deep-seated mental conflict in Mrs. Brightman's case, one which had been of long duration. It seems to have started after the death of her son and to have been in some way connected with it. From some reason, also, she seemed to be fearful that something in her life was responsible for his death, perhaps that his death was God's punishment of her. She seemed, too, to be connecting all this in some way with the attitudes of suspicion toward her on the part of his relatives. Why, also, was she so interested in the Portuguese girl who was suspected of illicit relations? Could it be that there was some question about the paternity of the boy who died? Those had been times when she was taking frequent trips alone to the city and enjoying a gay life. Her appreciation of the kindnesses of her manifestly unsuspecting husband and some seeming embarrassment it sometimes appeared to give her, would suggest as much. Was it possible that she had these many years been carrying that secret and sense of guilt? Might this be the source of her illnesses, so many of which seem to have been neurotic. Even the tuberculosis from which she now suffers, may have found opportunity to get its hold because of the weakening of her resistances through these many years of worry. That hypothesis seemed a diagnosis which, if it were correct, would explain most of the facts Perkins had noted. They decided there was no question about one thing: that Mrs. Brightman had some burden on her mind which was figuring largely in her illness, and that it was highly important, both for her spiritual and physical welfare, that she be helped to uncover it to somebody, presumably to Perkins. He should therefore go back and try to help her to entrust it to him.

From time to time during the ensuing months Perkins sent reports to Alison of his visits and her remarks. Following are a few excerpts:

"Called to see Mrs. B. She had just had a visit from some of her husband's relatives, who she supposed hated her. They brought her some food delicacies. That was nice. Perhaps they had forgiven her. At least it helped her comb hate cobwebs out of her own mind toward them. She was determined not to let her mind get cluttered up again with old hatreds and distrusts."

"Visitors were present, but Mrs. B. managed to say she had written me a letter, then destroyed it. There was something in it she had long been wanting to tell me, but on re-reading it, she had decided not to trouble me with her worries. I told her I was sorry she destroyed the letter and to write me another. But she has not done so. Apparently she cannot bring herself to do it."

"When I arrived, Mrs. B. was sitting up, evidently having arranged things for a talk with me alone. After a little encouragement she tried to do so. But it seemed she could not bring herself to give the essential thing, whatever it is. She began by saying there was not much to tell. Then her mind seemed to jump to something else, and she said, 'I really did not do anything wrong that time. I did not know those men or what they were doing.' No one had any right to talk about her the way they did. She only hated people who wronged her by talking about her, etc. Her sentences were disconnected, jerked out tensely. I finally pieced together that she was telling of an incident a few years ago when some men were caught bootlegging. It seems she had been out horseback riding and had met some of them, as a result of which she thought people charged her with helping conceal their lawbreaking. We were interrupted so that she could not proceed."

(Much later; near the end of the visits).

"I found Mrs. B. in bed, waiting for me. She at once began talking about 'that woman' and the violets. Rambled on with disconnected sentences about a doctor's wife having charged her with undue interest in her husband. Tried to reprimand her through the Eastern Star. One morning there were three black hats on her doorstep; that was a masonic symbol. One day she went to town, and all along the road were little girls in pink bonnets picking violets, etc. All her talk was fantastic, evidently distorted thinking. When I left it was manifest that there was something she was trying desperately to tell me, but was not able to do so. Each time she gets near it, somebody comes in and that ends it all."

All this time Mrs. Brightman's illness was constantly getting worse, the tuberculosis gaining constantly, evidently aided by her state of mental anxiety. It now became quite evident that some change would be necessary if her life was to be saved. Perhaps if she could be placed in a sanitarium with adequate medical care, and where there might be a better opportunity for her to unburden her heart to the pastor, as she manifestly wanted to do, it might yet be possible to arrest the disease. Her family were much concerned and ready to do anything possible, but they were very poor and unable to do much.

Perkins, therefore, went to the state authorities and asked that she be taken into a near-by state tuberculosis sanitarium as a free patient. They agreed to accept her. However, it would be necessary to have an X-ray examination and report and the commitment papers from the local physician. Perkins secured the ten dollars necessary to pay for the X-ray and then went to see the physician, whose services had been provided by the welfare authorities, the family not being able to pay for them.

Perkins explained to the physician that he had been interested as the pastor and had repeatedly tried to see the doctor about the case previously, but had never been able to do so. He then told him of the opportunity to place Mrs. Brightman in the sanitarium and that he was prepared to furnish the ten dollars expense for the X-ray, if the physician would sign the commitment. Then the state would take care of her. But the physician made plain that he resented the pastor having interfered in the case, sneered at the suggestion that her mental state had anything to do with it, said it was just a case of tuberculosis, the woman was going to die anyhow and the family had never paid him for what he had done. He refused to help place her in the sanitarium and plainly showed his resentment that the pastor had, as he seemed to think, infringed on his preserves.

Shortly after this Perkins was called away for a period of some months from his field. Before going he went to tell Mrs. Brightman of his going. She was greatly distressed, and seemed to become entirely despondent. To his efforts to cheer her up and his assurances he would see her after his return, she only shook her head. Her last hope was gone. Her spirit was broken. Within a month she died.

Both Alison and Perkins were deeply impressed with the significance of this case in many other ways than its tragic ending. It was evident now why Perkins had thought of the Adlerian approach in connection with it. For, while they both believed that the probabilities were that a sex offense had figured in the history of Mrs. Brightman, yet manifestly sex was not the dynamic force in her distress. It would be much nearer the truth to say that her urge for self realization, for making for herself a place in the world, was what led her into the associations in which her offense occurred, and that her subsequent troubles came largely in connection with her efforts to the same end in later years.

And yet that was not all. Greater still, was her yearning to escape from a sense of guilt and to find an adjustment with the larger world, with God himself. She felt herself out of tune with God's universe, she was torn by consciousness of something false within her, and until that was adjusted, naught else could avail. Only religion could have saved her. And it never got a chance.

Roxanna

It so chanced that while this case was going on Alison found himself at work on another which involved some of the same basic factors, and which lent further support to their sense of the importance of religion in such attempted adjustments. In this also there was a strong sense of guilt with fears and anxiety, and there was a gratifying cure through religious experience.

Roxanna was a young woman of thirty-six, divorced from a deserting husband, the mother of two children, eight and ten years old. Possessed of a small amount of property and a small income, she supplemented this by working in a relatively easy office position. The family lived in a respectable apartment. The children were in school.

Roxanna became confined to bed with paralysis of her left leg and lower torso. The paralysis was both sensory and motor. Needles could be pushed into her flesh freely without her knowing it and apparently the leg could have been amputated without pain. She had no muscular control over the affected parts. Expert medical examination disclosed no organic cause whatever and the case was diagnosed as hysteria. On the advice of the attending physician the services of a psychiatrist were secured but with no benefits resulting. The condition remained unchanged for several weeks. On the advice of Dr. Rogers with whom the attending physician was consulting, Alison was called into the case.

While Roxanna was not a member of Second Church, her children attended the Sunday-school. Dr. Rogers explained the case to Alison and told him of grounds he had for feeling that there was probably some moral or spiritual elements involved which the psychiatrist had not been able to adjust.

Alison proceeded to make pastoral calls on the woman. At first there was a manifest uneasiness on her part in his presence, and a tenseness which indicated strongly that there was something on her mind which his presence was disturbing. At the same time she made it evident that she appreciated his calls, and she seemed reluctant each time to have him go, as though there was something she wanted to say. Gradually her confidence increased, then suddenly one day, she broke out with it all in what the psychiatrists would call a full and free catharsis.

For some time she had been carrying on a liaison with a married man. Brought up in a rather strict Victorian atmosphere and with strong religious convictions regarding sex irregularities, she had a distressing feeling of guilt. Several times she had tried to break off the relationship, but she was not of strong character and the man involved was always able to overcome her resistances so that the relationship continued. As she now made her confessions to the minister, she revealed acute feelings of guilt and fear and anxiety: guilt because she had violated her moral standards, fear that by so doing she had lost favor with God and become a lost soul, anxiety because experience had led her to where she despaired of being able to break off a relationship she had now come to regret.

Alison, by his manifest understanding and utter absence of any attitude of censure, shock or blame, helped her tell the whole story. There was, of course no suggestion of condonement or approval. The whole approach was one of trying to help a distressed soul. Gently and sympathetically he led her through a series of spiritual experiences in which she came to an assurance of the forgiveness and fellowship of God and of strength from Him wherewith to carry out the new resolves of her heart. Immediately after this her condition manifestly changed. The drawn features relaxed, the frightened, hunted look disappeared from her eyes, she seemed restful and at peace. Alison said, "I think you are better." She replied, "I know I am!" Alison added a few words of further assurance and left the room. Shortly after he left she arose and dressed. Two years have since elapsed and there has been no return of the paralysis.

Alison was himself deeply impressed by this remarkable cure which he had not himself anticipated, at least in this striking form. Why had he succeeded when both physician and psychiatrist had failed?

Dr. Rogers and he agreed, as they discussed the case, that the explanation was evident. The paralysis was an hysteria and, like all hysterias, of psychogenetic origin. In this particular case, the source lay in combined feelings of guilt, fear and anxiety resulting from conflict between her extra-marital practices and her moral idealism and religious convictions. This conflict she had tried to drive out of her mind, but had only repressed it into her subconscious where it festered into a complex and emerged in paralysis. The paralysis relieved her from the conflict to the extent that as long as it continued she was free from temptation to repeat the offenses which she had felt powerless otherwise to resist. When the minister helped her into religious experiences whereby the guilt, fear and anxiety were removed, the complex was thereby resolved and the paralysis disappeared.

The particular locus of the paralysis interested them, as presenting a scientific question which the doctors were unable to answer without further inquiry, which they felt it would be unfair, at least for the present, to make of the patient. In some way the mind in its unconscious processes had attached the guilt feelings to the affected parts of her body and they became paralyzed. One was reminded of Jesus' words concerning a member of the body which shall cause one to offend, "Cut it off, and cast it from thee!" By her paralysis she had done so. Alison as a physician hoped that some time he might learn more from her as to the cause of her attaching blame to her left leg. But Alison was content in knowing that a soul was relieved.

The physician's work on the case was now complete. But not so that of Alison. There was still the man involved, who, the woman knew, would now at once try to renew his attentions. Apparently he was without moral restraints in the matter and concerned only with selfish gratifications. Alison realized the relative weakness of the woman's character, and that it would be a heavy strain upon her new life plan and faith, if she had to face him alone. At her request, therefore, he met the man with her. At first the man was arrogant, as Alison had rather anticipated, resenting the minister having interfered in what he plainly indicated he felt was their own affair and none of the minister's business. It was evident that here was a case in which firmness must replace kindness. Alison showed him that this also can find proper place in the work of a minister. When the man saw that further molestation on his part would mean legal proceedings against him with possible arrest, at least exposure to his family and employer, his attitude changed. It is unfortunate that sometimes one must thus resort to a big stick. But thereafter he left the woman alone, and Alison and his church people gave her the support which weak characters need. "We that are strong ought to bear the infirmities of the weak!"

What impressed both Alison and Dr. Rogers in the cure of Roxanna, was the part that religion played in it. It was evident that the removal of the guilt, fear and anxiety had made it possible. But why had the psychiatrist been unable to do this? It would be idle to suggest that it was only because of the superior skill or personality prestige of Alison; he himself would be the first to repudiate that. What really mattered was that the woman was helped into a compelling religious experience in which a consciousness of forgiveness and renewed fellowship with God drove out distressing fears, released emotional tensions, and thus relieved the paralysis. The sources were definitely spiritual. The psychiatrist might have succeeded if he were a religious man with as much skill and training as the minister in leading a soul to God. In a very real sense the Master's words can be applied to a case like this; "This kind cometh not out but by prayer and fasting!"

Experiences like these convinced Alison that for both understanding and cure of many human ills we need something beyond Freud.

Mary Roberts

The realization that neither Freudian nor any similar process of interpretation is always adequate without the religious element was impressed the more on Alison as he used these scientific methods of analysis in dealing with the type of case commonly confronting a pastor in his ministry.

It was notably so with Mary Roberts. Nearly two years before Alison met her, there had been an accident in which her husband was suddenly killed, leaving her with three small children and practically no financial resources. Following the tragedy she had gone into a nervous collapse, confined for some weeks to her bed. Since recovery from that she had kept very much to herself, particularly keeping away from church and manifestly shunning the fellowship of church people. She was becoming increasingly morose, cynical, introverted. Her children found her irritable, exacting, often unreasonable. Dr. Rogers, who had been her physician through her illness, explained the case to Alison as one which was plainly psycho-genetic and in all likelihood involving basic disturbances of a spiritual nature involving religious needs.

Alison went to work on the case understanding fully that he would not be welcomed and that he was probably in for a prolonged process. But he understood, also, that this resentment was not against him personally, but against him as the representative of something the woman resented and which she was projecting onto him. That something was probably connected in some way with religion, and he must be careful to avoid antagonizing it directly, if he was to make his way into her confidence. Gradually he gained ground, finding one and another item of interest, such as some problem of her children, in which he was able to be of service and in which in every case he was careful to make manifest that he understood her attitudes in the matter and was fully appreciative of them. Religion he never mentioned except as it came in naturally in conversation, and then with no suggestion of any consciousness on his part that there was anything amiss with her in that regard. More and more, as he did so, her antagonisms toward him decreased and he realized he was coming to impersonate to her more that was agreeable and less of her projected antipathies.

Finally came the day of his opportunity. She began by frankly telling him of one of her resentments. He saw that she was watching closely for his reactions, prepared, if there was any indication of rebuke or condemnation, to close up at once and probably finally. But he was manifestly understanding, there was nothing either of pity or blame. She felt him out with another lead. Again there was the same understanding, with neither shock nor surprise. Then the dams gave way and the floods came.

Bitterly she poured out the contents of her wretched soul! How the shock of her husband's untimely taking had laid her low. How she felt the terrible cruelty of her bereavement, the injustice to her who had always tried to do right, and who had been so happy with him, the awful lonesomeness, the anxieties and responsibility for her children on herself alone, the wrecking of all her finest life phantasies, how she hated God because of it all! Yes, hated God! For God, if there is any God, had done her an awful injustice and she could not forgive Him! Go to church? Talk religion? From all that she wanted to keep as far as possible. It only struck the hurt and made it worse. Believe? She believed nothing and nobody! Iron had cut too deeply into her soul!

She was watching Alison with the breath-holding intentness of a wounded animal at bay.

Still he was not shocked, nor surprised, not ready to argue against her nor taking her assertions lightly, not even by the twitch of a facial muscle betraying rebuke or blame!

She could not hate a man like that, nor project her antipathies onto him. But she could trust him.

Then came the fountain of her tears. She was unhappy. Well she now realized that! Life was not worth the living. Were it not for the children she would long to end it all!

With the tenderness and understanding of any competent pastor, but with an understanding also of the deeper emotional elements involved, which his clinical training and experience had given him, Alison proceeded with his counsel of help. As he did so she became increasingly composed and was quite evidently following him emotionally as well as intellectually in coming to a better understanding of her situation. Because she saw he did not doubt that a satisfying solution could be found for her problems, she began to think so too. Because he believed her troubles came largely from her not having properly understood her situations and herself, she, too, began to face them with an open mind. One thing was certain: her own interpretations had not got her anywhere except into bitterness. She would go with him into a careful exploration of herself. Perhaps there, not with God, she would find what needed to be changed.

Alison was too wise to attempt too much in that one interview. Better to let there be time for processes to work themselves through. For the present, a few things only were to be sealed home tightly: The first of these was assurance that the problems will be solved. Faith and hope for that must be strengthened with all that can be given them from her newly born faith in him. Then must come transfer of that faith and hope to God, at least to the extent of assuming that after all she may have been mistaken and God is not to blame, since Alison evidently thinks so. And there were the questions about herself; most of them were only opened or in some instances vaguely suggested. It was for her to inquire into her own thinking until they could talk it all over again. In the meantime, they would both try to trust God and he, at least, would pray. She was not sure whether she could do that or not. She was glad he did not ask her to. But she was glad, too, that he did himself say a few words of simple confident prayer as he took her hand on leaving.

The next interview found her composed and evidently eager for it. Together they went over her situation under his interpretations. For the first time she was able to analyze her complex needs. Yes, there was a physical need; she could now acknowledge that to herself, since Alison faced it so undisturbed. That much of Freud she could understand. And she learned with real relief of the avenues of sublimation open for her, particularly with her children, as they were now interpreted to her. But she realized just as truly that this was not all. There was that awful loneliness that was something else again. That also took on a new understanding, when she was shown its components; partly a dependence which must find another support to trust, partly a longing for response which must find other counterparts, partly appreciative recognition and fellowship which must also be found in others. Was that all? No, there was something more. There was that load of fears and anxieties that had overwhelmed her because of the financial and other responsibilities she now was forced to shoulder alone. Somehow, she must find relief from them.

Now she could understand herself more clearly. After all, it did not appear that God was to blame. On the other hand, as she looked back over these dark months, there was much in them that indicated that God had perhaps been helping her along in spite of her resistances against Him. Now that she realized that her sense of dependence was one of her un-met needs, it was helpful to have Alison point out that "God is our refuge and strength, a very present help in time of trouble." And when she faced her fears and anxieties, it meant something she had never realized before to hear the invitation to "Cast your care upon him for he careth for you," and find that bolstered by the testimony of her pastor that others, by doing so, have found peace for their souls. One and another of the aspects of her life, as they faced them together that day, loomed up as a need which only an experience of God could satisfy.

God became real to Mary Roberts that day. No longer did she blame Him for what she had not understood hitherto, no longer did she hate Him. In her soul of soul, she loved Him and found satisfaction.

Robert Thompson

The Thompsons had been a problem on Alison's hands for nearly two years before he found the solution. For some time he dealt with the problem as one purely religious, a matter of an intense desire for spiritual satisfactions. Later he undertook to interpret it on a Freudian basis. In both he failed. Then, as he studied the record of these years one morning, illumination came. After that his course was clear.

The Thompsons were in their later thirties with two children, a son Brainard now fourteen, and a daughter two years younger. Thompson was a mechanic, regularly employed but at moderate wages. His wife had been a skilled comptometer operator before her marriage and still worked part time to help out the family income. All were members of Second Church.

Thompson was known as a religious enthusiast. For a time he would attend all the services, taking part actively in the young people's meetings and elsewhere when there was an opportunity for him to talk. He was given to making speeches on the importance of more holy living and deeper religious experience, always with an implication that others were failing to live up to the higher ideals he espoused. Then he suddenly stopped coming to Second Church, and it was learned that he had joined a rather extreme fundamentalist sect, a group inclined to be critical of other churches and claiming a much higher sanctification. In a few months he had left that group and had joined another, this time one that insisted on a vegetarian diet as a matter of religious duty. This diet he forced onto his own family, somewhat to their discomfort. After a few months of this fellowship, he left this group also and suddenly returned to Second Church where he again became very active. But in a short time he had once more changed his fellowship, this time to an immersionist group. Within a year and a half, Thompson had joined no less than five such other religious bodies, and then finally returned to Second Church. He had much to say about the "second blessing" and holier living. He did not even hesitate to criticize Alison's preaching, doing it, however, directly to Alison and in no unkind way. He was evidently sincere, though his naive assumption of superior ability to make such criticism was amusing to the minister, who took it all quite good naturedly.

Thompson had been reared in a farmer's family,

where he was one of five children including two brothers older than himself. Both of them are now successful business men. Thompson for some reason left school in the ninth grade and went to work, learning the trade at which he is now employed. One of his sisters is a high school teacher, the other holds a good position with a law firm in the city where the Thompsons reside. All seemed to be kindly disposed toward Thompson, and on several occasions some of them had furnished financial help to his family when his own resources were being strained.

The home life of Thompson and his own family was constantly more or less distraught. Mrs. Thompson had been reared in a Catholic home, but had joined Second Church with him subsequent to her marriage. She was a rather superior woman, well liked in the community and by her employers. She was of more than average intelligence, with considerable religious understanding. She followed her husband in his various wanderings from church to church, largely in an effort to keep peace in the home, but also with a sincere desire to find anything available there which might reduce their frictions. Alison was frequently invited to their home for dinner, where they always led the conversation into a discussion of their religious problems.

When Alison was working on the hypothesis that sex might be at the bottom of their troubles, and so the explanation might be Freudian, he had learned two things from Mrs. Thompson which seemed to be important. One was that Thompson, following each new religious experience with another group, would refrain from all marital intimacies for a time as something inconsistent with the holier life to which he had been aspiring. Then he would indulge his desires. Following such indulgences there was always a period of depression, when he would smoke cigarettes incessantly. But this smoking he would also come to consider wrong, so he would be thrown into another depression which would last until he found some other religious group with whom he had another religious experience, when the same round would start once more. There was evidently a close connection between these sex problems and Thompson's religious vagaries, but Alison was unable to determine what causal relation there might be.

The other matter disclosed by his wife had to do with Thompson's earlier life. Mrs. Thompson said that their marriage had been a secret one in another state, from which they returned to tell their families about it. Then Thompson's mother told her frankly that she felt her son should not have married her, because she knew that he had been having intimate relations with another young woman who had expected him to marry her, and it was not fair to this other girl. When Mrs. Thompson confronted him with this and asked him why he had not told her, he replied that it was because he was afraid she would not marry him if he did so. Alison wondered whether there might be a guilt complex lingering there. But efforts along that line also brought no adequate solution. There certainly was somewhat of a guilt feeling, but all of that situation, Alison became convinced, was also in the course of the line of results from processes the ultimate source of which was more remote, and had led both to the indiscretions and to the concealment of them.

One day when Alison was taking dinner with the Thompsons, there was a discussion of some features of unconscious emotional processes and Alison told a simple story about an instance of repressed hatred. Suddenly Thompson said, "Now, that's the reason for my attitude toward Brainard. The conditions when he was born, the way my wife's folks acted and everything, made me resent him. You have often asked me why I don't like the boy. Well, that the reason!" The boy said, "Well, I like that!" Soon he got up and left the table. When his mother expressed regret that Thompson had spoken as he did in the presence of the boy, he replied that he supposed he should not have done it, but that Brainard was being given a mighty good start, far better than he himself had been given by his parents, and the kid must not be allowed to become too cocky.

It was this last incident that suggested to Alison the real cause of Thompson's troubles. This, along with other features of the long story as he tried to envision it all that morning, with the aid of his memoranda made from time to time, led to one of those intuitive suggestions seeming to come directly out of the blue by which most discoveries are made. Further and careful checking up from many angles satisfied Alison that he now had the explanation.

Thompson was suffering from an inferiority complex. It was deeply repressed, probably harking far back in his life to conditions in his childhood. The way that his two brothers, who have been markedly successful in life, had seemed to him to be preferred over him in the home and had treated him as an inconsequential little boy, had doubtless figured in it. Also the fact that he had for some reason dropped out of school at the ninth grade probably had significance. Out of it all the boy had grown up with this suggestion of inferiority, against which he was in hot rebellion, crowded down deep in his emotional processes, where it festered into a vicious complex and had kept breaking out during these many years. That explained why he had seduced the other girl before his marriage; it was a way of demonstrating to himself that he was strong enough to overpersuade another. It explained also why he had concealed it from the girl he married. For he greatly admired her and knew that she was his superior in many ways, and he did not propose she should know this or anything else about him that might make him appear inferior. It explained his rude actions toward Brainard; he was becoming jealous of his own son who was showing superior promise to what his father had attained. Of particular interest was the way it explained Thompson's religious wanderings. For in every instance he had gone to some group in which he could claim to have attained a higher degree of religious experience than others; a clear case of compensation by which Thompson could feel that he was now superior. It explained in the same connection why he had treated his wife as he had done in the course of these religious meanderings. For he always insisted that she follow him to the higher levels he claimed to have attained, but when she did so and seemed to be reaching those levels, then he had to rush away elsewhere to demonstrate to himself once more that he was her superior. It explained his courses with her in matters of marital relations. It explained his criticizing the religious attainments of other people and even presuming to be capable of passing judgment on his pastor's sermons and religious life. All were forms of compensations, efforts to escape from any acknowledgment of inferiority. The whole picture became clear when viewed from this angle.

Alison was now satisfied he had the right diagnosis. Freud had not this time given the key. It was Adler, rather, though Alison did not ally himself with any particular school of mental analysis. But for this case, he now had his point of departure.

Religion came in when Alison began his plans for treatment. The processes for relief from an inferiority complex as practiced by therapists are quite generally familiar and were to Alison, who proceeded to follow them here. Only there is always the problem in such cases of enabling the sufferer to find adequate evidences of actual worthwhileness in his own life, which become real compensations for the inferiorities which he has now been enabled to recognize and accept. Here comes in the Christian doctrine that every man's life is a plan of God, and that there is a place in the divine economy of the ages which each of us is set of God to fill and which none other can do as well. When that conviction, grounded as it can be so solidly in the teachings of Jesus, is clearly understood and accepted, there is permanent relief from the inferiority feeling from which escape had been vainly sought previously in all the unrealities of phantasy compensations and false pretenses.

Beyond Freud is always Jesus.

V

STRAINING AT LEASHES

PROPHYLAXIS is more valuable than cure. Alison realized this is just as true in the spiritual as in the physical. Modern medicine with its constant and increasing emphasis on prevention of disease and discovering it in incipient stages when often easily arrested, is just doing what the Church in its field has tried to do these many generations. Only, here again the Church has too often been lacking in scientific approach, perhaps because its practices found their patterns in a pre-scientific age. But the new case work program in Second Church was projected with fully as much consideration for preventing childhood and youth from going astray as it was with reclaiming the wandering and lost.

Parent-child relations, particularly as they are under strain in modern life, Alison realized, constituted no small part of the problem with which this part of the work would be engaged. Scenes like "The Cotter's Saturday Night" are rarely possible under modern American conditions. But the values therein conserved around the family altar are just as vital, and must somehow be retained. In these inhere the wholesome parent-child relationship itself, which in both Jewish and Christian culture has traditionally been surrounded by a religious sanction. Alison and his people were convinced that no parent-child adjustments are adequate in which religion is left out, and that they should, therefore, receive constant attention in the church's new program. But here, too, the approach should be scientific and personal. Mere pulpit admonitions would not suffice.

He became particularly concerned over the problems rising during the years of later adolescence, the time at which youth strains at its leashes and seeks increasing independence. Here, he saw, was a natural conflict between two equally wholesome "wishes," as W. I. Thomas calls them; that for "Security" on the part of parents, and that for "New Experience" on the part of youth. It is but natural and proper that parents should be concerned that their children be secure, and, therefore, should themselves exercise as much control as seems necessary to this end. But it is just as natural and proper that youth should seek widening horizons and such freedom as is necessary to that end. The balancing of the two is not always a simple art, but one in which parents particularly quite commonly err, with results that bring anxiety and sorrow. The dangers in their relations outside the home against which the Cotter warned his bairns, were simple compared with those which give anxiety to parents today and which often cause undue tightening of leashes against which youth is prone to strain. And with these problems Alison's people were increasingly coming for counsel, usually to go away surprised to learn that in their own blindness they had unwittingly contributed to the very delinquencies they feared.

EDGAR L.

Mr. and Mrs. L. were worried about Edgar. He was a young man of twenty-four, personally likable, with a good school record, now employed by Leo, a cousin of Mr. L., in a retail hardware store. Leo had taken a liking to Edgar, and indicated that he would give the boy every chance to learn the business, perhaps some day be taken into partnership.

But of late Edgar was constantly getting into trouble. When sent on errands in the business, he would do other things than what he was instructed to do. He seldom returned at the time expected, usually coming later, perhaps having, on his own initiative, attended to some other matter. Some times he just loitered away the time with no apparent purpose other than not to come back as expected. He often became involved in his accounts with the firm, frequently was short in his change, quite commonly was out of money himself and borrowing from others. On at least one occasion he had helped himself to money from the cash drawer. He had become quarrelsome with other employees, particularly with the girls in the office. At the Y. M. C. A. where he had been a frequenter from childhood, he was also getting into trouble. Recently ten dollars with which he had been entrusted there disappeared, he could not tell how. Frequently he spent his lunch money and was without food, not seeming to know where the money had gone. At home when remonstrated with for all this, he was not resentful but did not seem to care.

At the suggestion of a young man who was a friend of the family and active in some of the projects of the new program in Second Church, an appointment was secured with Alison for the parents and the three of them came together. During the inquiry, in which the young man's knowledge of the family and his experience in other case work were of much value, the following significant facts emerged:

Mrs. L. was Edgar's stepmother, having come into the family when Edgar was six years old, his sister four. There were no children by this second marriage. Mrs. L. was an intelligent woman of fine character, deeply devoted to Edgar and his sister, both of whom she seemed to love as her own. Relations between her and Mr. L. were in every way congenial; there was no evident discord in the family. Edgar and his sister were quite devoted to each other with no evidence of jealousies between them.

Mrs. L. had always given her first attention to the care of the two children, Mr. L. being a traveling salesman and usually out of the city except week-ends. Family matters he left in her hands, she making all purchases and handling the family finances. She had seen to it that both Edgar and his sister were adequately supplied with clothes and had what she considered a reasonable amount of spending money money allotted them each week. She saw to it also that they had opportunity and necessary money to attend entertainments and social affairs of which she approved, and did not seem to have been irritatingly narrow about where they should go, provided only they first secured her approval. Being a step-mother, she seems to have been all the more solicitous that her mothering should be of the very best for these children in her care. When Edgar went to work, he brought her his pay envelope each week, from which she gave him what she felt was ample spending money for carfares, lunches and incidentals. From the rest she bought his clothes and deposited the balance in a savings account she had opened for him in a bank.

Why, under these good conditions, was Edgar becoming delinquent? All of the family were concerned about it, even Edgar himself, who frankly said he knew he ought not to act as he was doing but he did not know why he did so.

Alison's task was not an easy one. Here was a case he could easily understand. Mrs. L., with all her good qualities, was a despot. She was a benevolent despot, it is true, but nonetheless a despot. She ruled the household. She did it kindly, but she did it. What was more, she intended to continue to do so, doing it really because she enjoyed the exercise of power, though it would be impossible for her to realize that. She honestly thought it was purely because of her unselfish devotion to the others. Mr. L., being away from home most of the time, found the arrangement quite satisfactory. But Edgar and his sister were still occupying the position of children. All decisions were made for them by Mrs. L. Because she did love them, loved them perhaps with a deeper passion because she had no offspring of her own, and so was pouring out all the fulness of her affection on these two, she was finding a deep satisfaction for her own soul in having them under her care. This satisfaction she was not going to give up, so she was seeing to it that they remained thus subject to her maternal care. She would not let them grow up.

Against all this Edgar was in inward rebellion. As a young man of twenty-four, he wanted to be his own master, making his own life decisions. Apron strings were the most galling of fetters. Against repression his manhood revolted. At the same time his appreciation and love for his step-mother kept him from open rebellion. This fact, Alison saw, was quite an asset; it implied a basic nobility in Edgar on which to build. His various derelictions were oubreakings of this repressed urge for adequate self-expresson, for adventure in manly self-realization. They did not appear to be in the nature of punishment for his parents. Had that been so, the course to be taken would have to be quite different. But they were quite evidently just efforts at securing self approval through adequate, untrammeled self expression. Good intentioned as was Mrs. L., it was she herself who was driving Edgar into wrongdoing.

It was now for Alison so to interpret all this to the family as to secure Edgar's release from the hold-over infancy treatment, and yet to do it without wounding the soul of this really fine woman. Deftly he did this, getting the parents to see that Edgar's emerging manhood was seeking free expression and that the wrongdoings were the result of urges which, rightly directed, would be entirely wholesome. But they must now learn the lesson hard for all of us parents to learn, when we must surrender control of our children, when we must look at our former docile little one now becoming a man and say, "He must increase, but I must decrease!" Of course it hurts. All that is worth while in parenthood hurts. But because of the hurts it is the more worth while.

The program Alison outlined was quite simple. Henceforth, Edgar was to handle his own finances. Instead of turning over his pay envelope to Mrs. L. each week, he was to pay her some proper amount for room and board and toward the household expense. All the rest he should retain and take care of his own expenses. To Mrs. L.'s anxious protest that he might squander all his money some week and have nothing left for lunches, it was replied, "That's his affair. Let him go hungry!"

"But," she protested, "I just can't do that!"

"Just that you must do, if you want to help Edgar."

"But he might not have money for carfare!"

"Then let him walk. A little exercise of that kind is good for a fellow and he will not be so likely to do it again. Your job in this is to let him alone, be kindly, never interfering, treating him constantly as you would any other man for whom you do not feel responsibility."

The young man who accompanied them was also given a part in the program. He was to be a companion to Edgar, treat him as a fellow young man, help him perhaps to find some wholesome girl friend, talk with him on his business affairs as he would to another man interested in the business, not as a mere office boy running errands. Treat him as a man till he is compelled to treat himself as such.

The trio went away to carry out the plan, Mrs. L. evidently quite dubious, but all of them determined to follow instructions because they believed in Alison. Alison's chief concern was over Mrs. L. Would she be able to do it? It would not be easy. To surrender power one has enjoyed is one of the hardest tasks we do, one of the heaviest crosses we bear. To succeed in it, it sometimes takes much of the spirit of Calvary.

Harold Rollins

Sometimes home leashes are broken, that is, part of them, the visible ones. Then the boy (it is usually a boy) leaves home, perhaps becomes a wanderer, as tens of thousands of them did during the early Thirties. At first he breathes deeply the enjoyment of his new "freedom" from home restraints, indulges avidly his urge for adventure, challenges the world in the abounding confidence of his assumed manhood. Usually the good job he expected to get quickly, does not materialize; jolts do however, then his real tests begin to come. Some drift into crime, most just drift. Harold Rollins was one of the latter.

Harold was seventeen when he came under the influences of Second Church through the interest of young Mr. Teems, a skilled workman in a large manufacturing establishment. For nearly two years, from time to time he had been around the plant where

Teems worked, doing odd jobs for a while, then disappearing for a period, usually several weeks. Teems managed to get somewhat of the boy's confidence, though he was very reticent and slow to put trust in anybody. Others at the plant told Teems he would get nowhere in his efforts to make friends with the boy, he was simply undependable. Teems invited Harold to take supper with him and his wife at their home but the boy refused, saying he had already eaten (which was not true). A few days later, Teems hired him to wash the windows in his apartment and, while he was there, persuaded him to take lunch with him and his wife. After that his attitude somewhat softened and he would occasionally drop in during an evening and chat with them.

Teems talked the matter over with Alison. Already enough had been learned about the boy to show that here was a case that was going to take considerable time and careful handling. But Teems and his wife were energetic and intelligent young people who were rather challenged by what appeared a discouraging undertaking. It was agreed, therefore, that they would go to work with Harold, keeping in touch with Alison from time to time, and in this way try to arrive at some understanding of this reticent and self-concealing boy. Alison had by this time begun keeping case records, something after the practice of social agencies, making them, of course, highly confidential and keeping his files away from scrutiny by any who might be curious about them. He explained to the Teemses that he thought it would make for much more efficient work on their part if they would keep some notes and bring him brief written reports. This they readily agreed to do.

Their first report was made about a month after this arrangement was agreed upon. Others followed over a period of six months. These Alison filed in order. Following is a summary of the facts they contained:

Second month. Harold seems to enjoy the home atmosphere and to try to find excuses for coming to spend an evening with us. We therefore made an arrangement for him to take dinner with us twice a week, in return for which he was to wash dishes and do certain other little tasks for Mrs. Teems. He now talks much more freely and calls our place "home." He has told us that he hails from West Virginia. His mother died when he was eleven years old, and a short time later his father married a much younger woman, with whom Harold could not get along. There was constant bickering and quarreling. At thirteen he left home and has never returned. In a short time he was wandering up and down the Pacific Coast. For the past two years he has been in and out of this city. The Travelers' Aid has twice sent him back to West Virginia, but in each case he slipped away before arriving home and returned here.

Third month. Harold is quite cynical about religion. He is evidently fond of his father in many ways, though he refuses to communicate with him. Apparently the one thing he has against his father is his having married the present wife. Otherwise he esteems him. His father, it seems, does not like preachers or church folks, for some reason. Harold says his father used to go to church sometimes, but he did not hesitate to walk out in the midst of the sermon if he did not like something that was said. Harold seems to admire this independence of his father, and is probably unconsciously copying it. However, he has gone a few times to Second Church affairs and even to the preaching service. Just now he is helping in the preparations for a play soon to be given by the young people, but he says he will not attend it. He resents anything that appears to be done by anyone for his good. For example, when he was offered a free ticket to a musicale he refused, saying he hated classical music, wanted what we call cheap entertainment. He seems ever watchful for some effort to be helpful to him, even by subtle suggestion, and manifestly resents it. He refused to listen to a suggestion about helpful books to read. But a little later he said he would like to have something to read, and when told to help himself to our library, he selected a "Story of the Bible" and took it with him.

Fourth month. Harold has always been very reticent about sex matters, refusing to talk about them at all. He would get up and leave the room if the subject came up in ordinary conversation in which he was participating. Of late, however, his attitude on this has changed. He has become quite fond of Mrs. Teems, whom he seems to regard as a big sister and treats as such. One night he asked her how to proceed to get a date with a girl. He is also saving his money and has accumulated forty dollars which he gave to Mr. Teems to put on deposit for him.

He has also been attending church quite frequently.

He has now taken a room with the Teems and is boarding there.

Fifth month. Harold has confided to Mr. Teems that he had been given to sex irregularities; seemed to be giving this as an explanation of his previous refusal to discuss sex and girls. There has also been a marked change in his emotional reactions lately. Formerly he acted much as a child, while posing as a sophisticated man. For example, on slight pretext he would become angry and leave, then shortly afterwards he would return, saying nothing about it. He also reacted to anyone manifesting an interest in him much as a child would do. However, he is still very reticent about his own affairs. At no time has an effort been made to pry into them, however.

Men at the plant are chiding Mr. Teems for spending so much time with "that worthless kid!"

Sixth month. Harold is showing symptoms of an inner conflict of some kind. He sleeps poorly, gets up early in the mornings, saying he cannot sleep. Has been saying frequently that he is going away, but he never goes. He is much less self-centered and now often expresses regrets over the misfortunes of others; something he never did in the earlier months when he was here. He had come to show much more interest in attending church. He was particularly interested in attending communion service, which he did recently at considerable personal sacrifice.

by a negative transfer, adopting his father's attitude toward religion. It enabled them to see how fruitless ordinary endeavors to win Harold to religion must have been. But when his other entanglements were adjusted, his attachment to religion and the church seemed to be natural.

Charles Lawrence

Lawrence had run through a pretty messy career. He said so himself, when he was brought into Alison's study one evening on an appointment by a classmate of his college days, now on the staff of one of the local social agencies. He was a handsome young man of about thirty-six, attractive personality, evidently quite capable. After a few words of explanation by his friend who had come with him, he told his story.

"I came here this afternoon from Baltimore. This may surprise you, but I came to give myself up to the police. My friend here and I were chums in college, and I came here to tell him all about it before doing so. You see, I have led a wicked life for some years. I've been in jail before; eighteen months on a forgery charge. Well, that didn't change me. Since that I have forged other checks, stolen an automobile and done a lot of other things for which I never took the rap. Now, I didn't let it all bother me so long as I was not getting caught again, till a few days ago, when I met a fellow on a train who was returning from a meeting of what he called The Oxford Group. He told me that he had found God in a new way at their houseparty. Then he told me of some wrongful things he had done (they were small stuff compared with my record), and then said he was on his way back home to make what he called 'restitution.' The whole attitude of the fellow hit me hard. He seemed so radiantly happy, so transparently at peace with himself in view of what he was doing that I couldn't get him out of my mind. I haven't slept much since. All that he said about restitution gripped me, made me think about myself and feel that I ought to give myself up and take my rap. God became real to me as He never was before. God seemed so real to him I guess I sort of caught it from him. I want to go to jail now to make restitution for my crimes. I have to do that to get spiritual peace. But my old-time chum here isn't sure that's the thing I should do. That's the reason we came to you."

Further conversation brought out that Lawrence had quite a marital history; had been married twice, divorcing his first wife with whom he had two children and abandoning the second, who, he understands, is now getting a divorce, and after that living with a third woman to whom he is not married. Sex irregularities have been common since his break with his first wife. That followed closely upon the start of his forgeries and thefts. Prior to that he had conformed generally to conventional moral patterns. He had come from a devoutly religious upper middle class home with an excellent religious background, to which, however, he seems to have responded rather perfunctorily. He had a high intellectual rating, making a *cum laude* in college, and was always able to land good positions with salaries running in the thousands, but losing them for various reasons he could not explain, following which he usually resorted to forgeries which he had done without any scruple.

Alison at once understood why the social worker had brought this case to him. Here was a man in serious trouble that was not only manifestly spiritual, but which was directly religious. That is, his delinquencies rooted back into spiritual maladjustments which were so directly related to religion in his history that his experience with the Oxford Grouper had stirred up this deep emotional experience. It was distinctively a case for a minister of religion. He therefore made it plain at once that he would be glad to cooperate in an effort to help the man find an adjustment of his problems.

As to giving himself up to the police at once, Alison said he agreed with the social worker that it would not be wise to do that immediately, not at least till they had thought through a larger program. It could just as well be done later. Of course something must be done to attain the ends Lawrence had in mind, but perhaps that might not be the best way to do it. Better for us to think that through more fully. Just why should he give himself up to the police? To pay a debt to "society"? Was it really to "society" that he owed a debt, or was it to the particular people he had defrauded? Since his guilt was not yet known, had society outside his victims yet been injured? How far would he actually get in the way of restitution by going to jail? That would not repay what he owed individuals. And it would reduce the likelihood of his being able thereafter to get a position whereby he might make money to pay back what he had taken. Would it do society any real good to have himself thus exposed? Might it not be better to think in terms of restitution to those he had defrauded?

"But," said Lawrence, "I want peace in my own soul. I have sinned in this against God and I ought to go to jail. I believe that if I once get behind prison bars God will accept me. Then I might be able to testify there to other fellows who have gone wrong."

"Are you quite sure you would find peace with God in that way?" asked Alison. "You would still have the memories of unpaid debts on the outside. Frankly, I do not think that is the way for you to God. That is too much like the eastern dervish who cuts himself with knives to win God's favor. Making yourself miserable is not restitution."

Lawrence understood, and agreed to do otherwise if a better plan could be proposed. On Alison's suggestion, Lawrence agreed to go the next day to several men in the city whom he had defrauded, confess the whole matter to them and offer to make restitution as he might be able, or agree that they should have him arrested if they so preferred. In the meantime without telling Lawrence, Alison and the social worker managed in each case to get to the business men in advance, telling them about Lawrence and preparing the way for him. In a few cases where the business men hesitated, the social worker stated frankly to them that he had a personal interest in Lawrence, and offered to advance some money himself in the way of partial settlement. When Lawrence came back that evening, it was to report that not a single one he interviewed wanted him arrested. The way was clear, so far as they were concerned, for him to try to get a job and start making repayments. But how about others he had defrauded elsewhere? Fortunately, they were not so many. And, with Lawrence's earning ability, it was evident he could hope in a few years to pay all of them. He decided, therefore, that it would not be fair to the men who had treated him so well that day, for him now to do anything elsewhere that would spoil the situation. During the day the social worker had formed a contract which was followed up the next day and Lawrence secured a job. The pay was not large at first, but with Lawrence's abilities there was every likelihood that he would make rapid advancement.

That was the beginning of a course of fellowship with Lawrence that lasted two years before his spiritual reclamation was complete. He made good in a business way at once and soon was making sufficient money to start substantial payments on all his defalcations, including those in other states. In the meantime he had become a close participant in Second Church and its work. With the start of a practical program of restitution, his mind was set at ease. His desire to "confess," which had disturbed him so much in the beginning, Alison had helped him to analyze, till he saw only part of it was wholesome, and that part was fulfilled in his direct confessions to those he had robbed. Confession, Alison had insisted, should ordinarily be as widespread as the knowledge of the offense and no more so. The Kingdom of God is not advanced by parading our secret sins before the world, and there is a real danger that we may ourselves suffer spiritually by coming to enjoy bragging about how bad we once were.

But Alison had realized, too, that Lawrence's real spiritual problems were not to be solved by dealing only with his forgeries. After all, they were results; what were the spiritual sources? That led to a careful study by Lawrence, under Alison's direction, into his early life and particularly his marital history. The fact came out that his financial delinquencies followed upon strained relations which had developed between himself and his wife. More and more, as he studied his own record, he became convinced there was a connection between them. The conflicts which he experienced at home, he had tried to compensate for in some way by taking it out on others elsewhere. Then the difficulties into which that led him resulted in his later sex offenses, which were really unconscious efforts on his part to punish his first wife.

But what were the causes of his troubles with her? He could not now really say they were her fault. She was a fine woman whom he highly respected and who, he knew, had deeply loved him and still did so. Their marital relations had not always been fully satisfying to him, but he realized now that might have been overcome by better understanding. Yet he had himself grown to resent his marital ties, grown increasingly restless, and finally broken out in the delinquencies from which his further troubles had followed.

It was one more case, Alison saw, of straining at leashes. Only this time, so deeply involved that the real cause was concealed entirely from himself. Lawrence had been well conditioned before his marriage under constant parental care. He had been given apparent freedom to make his own way in life, but always there was the protecting watchfulness of his parents ready to come to his rescue if needed. He had perfect freedom for everything except to fail. He might go anywhere he wanted to go except that he could not go to the devil; their watchful care would prevent that. Then he had married and his wife and own home support became a surrogate for the same loving restraints. Against these his spirit of adventure was in constant protest. He could no more be content to adventure merely within the limits of safety, than can the sportsman be satisfied with sports in which there is no real danger. His wife as well as his parents symbolized this restraint. He would deliberately break over. His free spirit would find escape. Crime was the way.

All this Alison had to interpret to Lawrence, doing it gradually and chiefly by so directing Lawrence's own thinking that he found it out for himself. As in all such cases, bringing the complex thus into open consciousness destroyed its vicious power. The urge for adventure, having thus vindicated its claim to freedom, ceased to find crime attractive as a path of expression. More than that, the old love for his wife, against whom it had led him to rebel, now came back. There were mutual interpretations and understanding, they have been remarried and their home happily reestablished. It was only by thus providing release, however, that this could be done. Without it, the most that could have been accomplished would have been a life-long armistice.

Religion, Lawrence himself came to see, had figured at the very heart of his troubles and was essential to their adjustment. Religion had been the sanction of all the moral restraints in childhood and later in his own home. It was religious sanctions, then, in the last analysis, against which he had been in rebellion. That was the reason his releases were coming in the same way. When he met that Oxford Grouper, two things struck home to his inner soul; first, the fact that this man had manifestly arrived at the goals of satisfaction in life which he himself had unsuccessfully sought by courses of crime, and; second, that he had found it by submission to the very restraints against which Lawrence had all these years waged rebellious war. God had "suddenly become real to him," and he came to "see God in a different light." The urge for restitution was a new rebellion on the part of his own soul, this time against the pulls which had thus put him into antagonism with God. Adjustment was accomplished by his coming to where he could accept the restraints which now he saw as wholesome guides to self-directed conduct. And God became an accepted and appreciated part of his realistic world.

VI

SINS UNPARDONABLE?

ARE there any hopeless cases?

Alison knew that social workers generally assume there are. They do not call them that; it is much more comfortable to call them "closed" cases and imply they may, perhaps, be somebody else's responsibility. But as a Christian he hesitated. He liked to think in terms of a "whosever will" gospel; that God is not willing that any should perish and neither should a Christian worker be. On the other hand, he remembered that there were those for whom even his Lord said He did not ask us to pray, presumably because they were beyond redemption. Beyond redemption, Alison believed, only because they had reached the place where for some reason they were unwilling to be changed. Had not the Master lamented about such, "Ye *will* not come unto me that ye might have life?"

Maxine had seemed such a case. And there were others.

PRUDENCE L.

One such was Prudence L. Alison had known her and her family situation intimately for years and had dealt with it without avail. Prudence still continues the same, or rather, both she and the situation seem to grow continually worse. And the worse it becomes, the more gratified Prudence seems to be. That is the disheartening part of it all.

Prudence is a married woman of approximately fifty years, wife of a high school principal, mother of two daughters, one of them married. She is physically attractive and ordinarily of good health, but with hypochondriacal tendencies. Her early life was spent in a small town where she attended school through junior high school grades. Early home conditions were generally good, though her childhood was somewhat dominated by an older sister of stronger character. Married in early twenties, since that time she has lived in larger towns and cities where her husband has been engaged in teaching. She is of the motor-minded type, seldom reads more than headlines and advertisements, is not interested in literature, though somewhat in art, in which she has good taste. Such mental tests as have been possible indicate an I.Q. of approximately seventy-five to eighty. Her conversation is limited to commonplaces with little participation in group discussions.

Prudence is dominated by an intense jealousy, first of her husband and now extended to numerous others. The onset, so far as Alison has been able to learn, occured many years ago, seven or eight years after her marriage, and in connection with a certain literary society before which her husband had been invited to read a paper at a meeting at which she was present. The paper was well received and was followed by an appreciative discussion in which her husband was a stellar figure, but in which she was unable to participate because the subject matter was clearly beyond her grasp. This fact she seems to have realized, together with a realization that other women present did understand and were able to participate in the discussion intelligently. Prudence seems to have sensed her inferiority and to have resented it greatly. Her resentment was manifested quite evidently at the time, and was carried over into her attitude against her husband and others participating in the discussion. The incident itself appeared insignificant to the others at the time, but seems not to have been so with Prudence. For the first time in her life, she was forced to face evidences of inferiority on her own part which stung her to the depths of her soul. Probably memories of the earlier dominance over her by her stronger sister, which as a child she had resented, and from which she thought to have escaped through marriage, figured also in her revolt against this seemingly new humiliation, and she rebelled against it all. The result was a repression into her unconscious levels, where an inferiority complex developed which has grown through the years.

Prudence's jealousy is a direct expression of her inferiority complex, as jealousy so commonly is. Her husband became its direct object, because it was his attainments that night which had revealed her inferiority to her. And every success he achieves in life, every recognition given him, only feeds it the more. In later years she has come to transfer it also to others of her friends who attain distinctions of any kind. Success or recognition for any of them is likely to be the signal for an antagonism on the part of Prudence, so that she alienates many of them from her. At first her resentment expressed itself in mere poutings, then in open fault-finding, quarrelsomeness, then temper tantrums. As years passed it became more and more sadistic in manifestations, till she seemed to find life's chief satisfactions in making others, particularly her husband, suffer. In more recent years there were increasing evidences of character disintegration. There was notable compensation in the way of self-approval. It came to seem impossible for her to believe she was ever wrong or ever made a mistake. Self-pity was constantly to the fore. Increasingly she lost power to control her emotions, any one of which was likely to run riot till there was exhaustion. Disturbed intellectual processes were manifested in her prevailing type of conversation, which was a constant flow of chatter unrestricted as to association of ideas, beginning with some statement in which a word or sentence would suggest another idea to which she would turn, only to have this repeated with some other suggestion, thus rambling on and never returning to the original subject. She became suspicious of approaches, more and more persistent in sadistic petty persecutions, apparently finding her chief satisfactions in the discomfitures of others.

How was Prudence to be helped? Alison did not know. The heart of the trouble was that she manifestly did not want to be changed. Hers was a dark situation. She seemed to love the darkness rather than the light.

William the Conqueror

Alison dubbed him that in his own thinking. For he was a "successful" business man who had arrived at wealth and power by ruthless crushing of others, and who gloried in it. Even the hatred he knew was felt toward him by the victims of his shrewd exploits seemed to feed his self-satisfaction.

William had started in life with the world seemingly arrayed against him. The son of a dissolute father and a mother who compensated for her sufferings from her husband by tyrannizing over her children, and laughed at by other children because of a rather unattractive countenance, William had set himself in childhood to conquer the world which he resented for its cruelties to him. He fought his way through the situations in the playground. He fought his way through sports and classes in high school and technical courses. He fought his way into business and on through all his succeeding years. Today he had arrived at the head of an important financial organization controlling several industries and employing hundreds of men, over all of which his word was supreme. Any one he could not master he hated. Anyone he could, he despised.

How could the love of God find lodgment in a heart like that? Alison did not know.

Diagnosis of the case was relatively easy. Anyone

could see that what William was had come most naturally out of the reactions of the strength with which he had been endowed against the antagonisms of life as he had experienced it. But that was of little help in deciding what to do in the way of helping the man into Christian experience. "All the fitness he requireth," said an old hymn, "is to feel the need of Him!" But that was just the trouble. William did not feel the need of anyone outside himself. He could unhesitatingly smite his breast and shout "I am the captain of my soul!"

William was not a member of any church. Alison might have secured him for Second Church, had he been willing to go with abject fawning and ask him to honor the church with his patronizing membership. But that was one thing Alison would never do. He would not, because to do so would be still more damning to the man's arrogant self-worshiping soul. Much as Alison wanted every worthy support for Second Church, he would not try to build it up by support secured at the cost of strengthening still more the very resistances which must be overcome if William were to know the joys of real Christian experience. William knew Alison and did not like him because he did not fawn upon him as did others. Alison knew that. But he dared not do it. To do so would be to betray his Master. On the other hand, he was careful not to do anything at which William could properly take offense. That was in the hope that, perhaps through trouble, William would come to a sense of need and then there might be a chance to help.

But would that time ever come? It might. But Alison well knew there are not a few cases in which it does not. The blessings of adversity are not always vouched to arrogant men. Some of them pass on to life's end without them. It might be so with William. In the meantime, what could be done?

Alison did not know. He could only wait.

Cases such as Maxine, Prudence and William did seem beyond redemption. At least Alison had not succeeded with them and saw no prospect of doing so. He knew social workers who would cross them off their list. He remembered how Adler dismissed a patient whom he found secretly cheating, and how Hartwell declared he could do nothing with a boy who would not be honest with him, and how Ewer declares that "an indispensable precondition of success is a sincere desire to conquer" both the indisposition and its cause. But as a Christian worker, Alison could not bring himself to be content with this. Religion, he felt, looks for its opportunity in beginning where other agencies give up in despair. Was not the whole of Begbie's *Twice-Born Men* the story of successes just of that kind? Does not our Bible present God as saying "I will take away the stony heart, and give you a heart of flesh"?

So far as anything Alison had secured from his clinical studies in social and psychiatric work could show, there was nothing of promise for cases such as these. From his religious background it was not so hopeless. For while social workers look for the cooperative attitude, religion undertakes to produce it. But how was this to be done? William James had found, in his study of the varieties of religious experience, that religion produces the change of attitude found in "conversion" by "a certain form of deliverance" which consists of two parts: an uneasiness rising out of a sense that there is something wrong with us, and a release from the uneasiness by an experience of being saved from the wrongness through making proper connections with higher powers. But how were these people to be brought to such an "uneasiness"? The Christian way, he saw, was by confronting one with a superior ideal as seen in the Christ and as reflected in His followers, and thereby destroying the self-approval that had been satisfying. But how impress them with that superior ideal as long as their distorted taste preferred the very unchristlikeness that distorted them? Verily, as the Master said, having thus taken of their old wine they do not straightway desire new for they say the old is better! Even as a Christian worker, he can only wait.

But this did not mean that these cases were "closed." In Christian work no unadjusted case is ever closed, no client dismissed because uncooperative. The fruitless tree is still to be digged about and, perhaps, deftly fertilized. Christian faith ever trusts, with the Wesleys, that "While the fire remains to burn, the vilest sinner may return," and in that hope continues watchfully to wait.

And yet that was not all. None of these cases was as simple even as this. For in every case there were family involvements and not a little discord. What should be done about them?

Should Prudence be encouraged to go ahead with the divorce proceedings, of which she talked much but which Alison surmised she did not really want? The discord in that home was certainly bad for all of them, but was divorce the solution? Alison was not orthodox on the divorce question as some churchmen count orthodoxy. He applied the Master's dictum that "The Sabbath was made for man and not man for the Sabbath" to other institutional relations, including marriage. He did not consider divorce so much a cause of a broken home as a result of it. He did not believe that anything wholesome is conserved by holding people bound together in the interests of an institution, at the cost of such discord and other evils as may do irreparable harm to the souls involved. But would divorce in this case bring benefits greater than its costs? He realized that Prudence would have been more happy, would probably have never suffered her emotional reverses, if she had married a man of a mental calibre more like her own. That, of course, was one of the unfortunate features of her history. But the fact was she had not so married, and now has to deal with the marriage she did make. He did not believe that she would be relieved of her emotional disturbances by being divorced, or that she really desired it. Her antagonisms against her husband were in the nature of an ambivalence toward one to whom she was so emotionally tied that separation would only increase her difficulties within herself. She both loved and hated him, and would continue to do so even if she were to secure a divorce and marry another. The only escape from her miseries must be through a change within herself, which at present seems to be the one thing she does not desire.

But how about the other members of the family, particularly her husband? For Alison did not forget that he had just as real pastoral responsibilities to them as to her. In that regard his position was somewhat different from that of the psychiatrist, who is prone to think chiefly in terms of his responsibility for the patient, and is sometimes tempted to sacrifice others to help the patient. He remembered a case where a psychiatrist, who was undertaking very earnestly to rehabilitate a dissipated roué, now in his later thirties and broken in health through long excesses and two venereal diseases, actually tried to persuade a clean, inexperienced young girl of eighteen to marry the patient! As a pastor he must think just as much in terms of the spiritual welfare of the other members of Prudence's family as of herself.

But would divorce relieve the situation for Prudence's husband? He doubted it. More likely, he felt, would the man go out with a feeling of defeat and somewhat of guilt over a tragic ending of their marriage, in which he could but remember that he had been the superior one in capacities, and therefore in responsibility for making the marriage a success. Perhaps, also, he would find the situation to be one challenging him to an enduring and sacrificing attitude, from which he could not turn aside without another cause for feeling failure and defeat. History is not without examples of this kind. Alison remembered the incident in the life of Abraham Lincoln when Mr. Lincoln was in the midst of an important conference with a cabinet officer and Mrs. Lincoln broke into the room with one of the tirades to which she was frequently given in some of her temper tantrums. When she had stormed out of the room, the cabinet officer said to Mr. Lincoln who had not spoken while she was there, "Mr. Lincoln, why don't you shut her up?" Mr. Lincoln replied, "What would be the use? She seems to enjoy it, and it doesn't hurt me any!" He recalled also the story about the sainted John Wesley, that once the aged man was seen actually being dragged on the floor by his flowing white hair in the hands of his temper-crazed wife, and yet who was never known to have mentioned her abuses to anyone. Whether Prudence's husband was big enough to emulate Lincoln and Wesley he did not know. And whether he should be encouraged to continue to endure he did not know. There were some evidences that the man's health was breaking under the constant strain. Should that also be sacrificed to Prudence's ego-centricity? Here were questions not yet to be answered. Alison continued to wait, watchfully wait.

With William the situation was different, but likewise complex. For he too had a family, over which he tyrannized without stint. His wife was of a submissive type that did not particularly resent it, and who had an artful way of wielding him to her purposes without his knowing it. But his growing son had much of the father's disposition and conflict was already in sight. Then there were the men in his employ, particularly workingmen, who deeply resented his domineering attitudes. Here Alison saw the seeds of discontent which needed only time to ripen into bitter labor disputes, and possibly larger social disturbance. And these workingmen, too, were part of the community with which Alison's responsibilities were concerned. William was a social menace by virtue of the personality defects which his lack of religious experience and Christian character entailed. Here again, no adequate adjustment was in sight. But here also, as a Christian worker, he could not dismiss the case as hopeless and closed. Whether William would successfully persist in his arrogant selfishness to the end, time alone could tell. But in the meantime, the spiritual interests of these other persons must be conserved. That also was part of the task.

VII

FROM CURE TO PREVENTION

ALISON had made it plain when inaugurating the new clinical program that it was in no sense to be a one-man affair on his part. He saw clearly that such an effort would quickly swamp him in a mass of detail, only a small part of which any one man could administer. He realized just as much that the whole enterprise could succeed only as it enlisted the active participation of a goodly corps of members of the church in the kind of ministeries he had been describing. Hope for its success rested upon a conception of the church much akin to that of early apostolic times, when they that loved the Lord were together as a cooperative group all participating in a common enterprise. Under a pulpit-centered and sermon-dominated conception of the church, a member might perhaps feel that his part had been performed when he supported the preacher financially and otherwise, but not so with this kind of a program. Giving the gospel to the people of a community under this conception was not something a congregation could hire a man to do for them. Only by active participation themselves in spiritual ministries to individuals with whom they might be brought into contact in connection with their life problems, could the members of Second Church furnish the support without which the whole enterprise could not succeed. Fortunately there was much in the history of Second Church to support this idea of the minister being a sort of "human engineer," whose work was in no small part that of an executive planning and directing programs in which many participated. Alison had capitalized this in presenting his new program. The people took pride in the record of their church as a working church and Alison was thus turning this into another kind of expression.

The people had responded in a most gratifying way. Several, such as Mr. and Mrs. Teems, Dr. Rogers and others of large understanding, were early drawn into participation with the pastor in programs of service to individuals as instances of need appeared. The work had not gone long, however, till it became quite evident that the people of the church generally were much in need of education and training for the tasks they were now asked to undertake. Very few of them, for instance, could have handled the situation with Harold Rollins as the Teemses had done.

This was not because they were an ignorant people. On the other hand, they were people of relatively high intelligence and understanding of current conditions and problems. In traditional lines of religious education also, the Bible, its history and doctrines, the history and work of church missions and general church enterprises, Second Church enjoyed an exceptional record. But when these same faithful church people were confronted with tasks rising in the new clinical approach, many of them were puzzled. They were not skilled in analysis, either of the social situations or of the psychological reactions of the individuals they were asked to help. Still more, they had very hazy ideas about the particular functions which religion might be expected to perform in helping people in the situations with which they had to deal. They knew better than most people the statement of the church creeds about the salvation of mankind in general, but when it came to how the grace of God is to be made effective in this disrupted home, with that erring boy, with yonder distracted girl, well, that was something quite different. For that kind of service they were poorly prepared.

Alison saw that he had an educational job on his hands in this. He recalled how, a couple of years before, when he was a board member of the Family Welfare Society, the General Secretary had conducted a training school for volunteer workers. At the time he had noticed that many of them were church people, including not a few from his own church. He had often thought about that since, and asked himself how it came about that these church people were so uneducated in this way, and why the training had not featured their preparation for work in their own churches in which there was so much need of the very kind of friendly support and counsel there being emphasized. He could not escape the conviction, too, that better service could commonly be rendered if there were included an intelligent cultivation of religious life, something which a non-religious agency, responsible primarily for other interests, generally felt to be outside its province. Alison now set about to educate and train his people for this service.

In consultation with his official board, whom he always took into counsel before launching any proposal, not only as a matter of strategy but because he had found their viewpoints often of great value, it was decided to use some of the evening services for this purpose. Second Church had been slow to follow the practice of many others in abandoning the evening service entirely. But the attendance had been small, practically confined to the more earnest and faithful members of the church itself. He had already departed from making the evening service a replica of that of the morning, and had begun introducing special features. It was now decided to extend this still further and devote these evenings for a few weeks to adult education in the application of the Christian gospel to the life situations of individuals.

Announcement to this effect was made in a Sunday morning service. Alison alluded to the fact that problems of social reconstruction and programs for world betterment are quite commonly discussed in churches at their Sunday evening meetings, all of which he believed to be proper and had no doubt that something similar would be done at Second Church from time to time. But these immediate programs were something different. In the first place, they were being planned primarily for the workers already in the church and for the young people who are to be its workers tomorrow, though others would of course be welcome. The immediate objective had to do with making the work of the church more effective now in helping individuals make the best of their situations, without waiting for the more elaborate but slower processes of social reconstruction.

It had been agreed in the board meeting that the whole sermon period of that morning service should be devoted to the subject, several members of the board insisting this should be done. In doing so, Alison made plain to the people that what was wanted was not merely that they should enjoy one or another of the lectures to be given. Rather, he urged that they should be taken with the same seriousness as any other training course on which one might enter in some professional or vocational school. Each lecture was to be followed by a discussion period, and the whole would be very closely related to the types of problems with which they were dealing in everyday life round about them. Out of it all those who attended were to expect to come better equipped for the new work of the church, for which they are showing such a splendid enthusiasm. At the same time, he warned them that the training into which they were being invited, was not something to be achieved quickly. What he hoped to accomplish was, first, to make clearer just what religion itself could be made to mean in a given life situation, and second, to set forth some of the techniques needed for the less intricate parts most of them would be undertaking in the work as it proceeded in the community. He then called attention to the printed programs, already distributed in the pews, for the first series of four Sunday night lectures with which the project was to be launched the following week.

"Psychology and Salvation" was announced as the general subject for these lectures. Alison explained that they were planned to furnish a background from which each one would be better able to understand the life situations with which he would be dealing, and some of the things he might be asked to do in connection with them. The first night he was greeted by an audience containing the majority of his dependable workers, together with a goodly number of young people, most of whom continued with him through the series. The second night they began participating freely in discussion, chiefly in the way of raising questions which had come up in connection with their own experiences in the church's new program. By the end of the series the new régime was under way. There was still a long way for these people to go before they would be skilled therapists of the soul. But they now knew where they were trying to go.

Then something else happened.

Second Church had the traditional Sunday-school, of which Mr. Martin, a teacher of history and social science in the nearby high school, was superintendent. Mr. Martin had taken charge of the Sunday-school something over a year before on request of the official board of the church. Like many others of the time, the school was steadily losing ground, and he had been asked to take charge in the hope that he might suggest changes which would be helpful. He had made changes in curriculum and secured some helpful additions to the teaching staff, but the attendance continued about the same. Near the close of Alison's series of Sunday evening lectures, Martin asked for a conference, the outcome of which was to have far-reaching consequences in the program of Second Church.

"I have reached the place," said Martin, "where I am convinced our whole program of religious education in the church is in need of reorientation. As you know, I have been trying during the last year or so to improve our school by the introduction of various modern changes in curriculum and program. But the results have not been encouraging. The more I study the situation, the more I have come to the conviction that we need an entirely different kind of approach. Our change in the program of the church itself to this clinical emphasis has helped me to see the responsibilities of the school in a different light. You have helped us to see the church's work as primarily a ministry to the health of souls rather than the delivery of a message. I have reached the place where I believe the same situation should obtain in religious education. We should see it as a project in spiritual prophylaxis for the nurture and promotion of the growth of the child's spiritual life.

"Of course, I know that modern education has taken on a great deal of this character, and some of it has come over into the religious education programs of the church, but not very much as yet. We are still pretty generally oriented from the viewpoint of a set of messages to deliver, just as we used to be in the work of the church itself. I do not mean for a moment to minimize the fact that we have a message and that it is important. But I think it should figure with us as it does with you in your program, something on which to draw to meet the needs of a person as we find them.

"I had heard of an experiment undertaken in one of the churches in another city along the lines in which I have been thinking, and I recently paid a visit there to study it in operation. I came away convinced they have found the proper approach. Now I want to tell you what I think our program should be. I, of course, realize that it cannot all be instituted at once. But here, as I see it, is our goal:

"We should provide ourselves with a spiritual child clinic, just as our parents have become accustomed to having a child health clinic. I found this in the church I visited. They were fortunate in having access to a psychological department in a nearby college which furnished much of the service, advanced students participating in it much as medical students do in our own child health clinic here. An interesting set of tests had been devised, and mothers brought their small children there, just as they did to the child health clinic. The children were tested as to their aptitudes and attitudes and each mother was given a prescription for the nurture and care of her child's spiritual life and growth, precisely as is done for the physical diet and care of a child at the health clinic. I found that more than three hundred children had been brought for such tests and instruction. That meant that every one of those mothers could start the religious nurture of her child with as much knowledge concerning its spiritual needs as was the case with her care for its physical health and growth. That, you see, is just applying in religious education the policy of personal diagnosis you have been using in your ministry."

"One thing I like about your idea," said Alison, "is that it puts the religious education job back to the parents in the home."

"Precisely," Martin replied. "I know, and you know, that something was lost when the Cotter's Saturday Night gave way so commonly in America to an hour for the children at Sunday-school, while the parents gave their thoughts to other things. I believe this is part of the way to bring back those values in different form today.

"Now, here is where the change in the school comes in; these children are grouped in the school on the basis of like aptitudes and attitudes, as they have been disclosed in the tests. In other words, the very principles which advanced pedagogy is following in our public schools are being applied here. Only, in some regards, I believe we are in position to go even farther in this than the limitations of the public school permit."

"I think I see what you have in mind," said Alison, "concerning the small children. But how about those who are older?"

"I have not yet reached a place where I have as specific ideas for them as for the little children, but I believe the same principles should obtain. That is, we should be carrying the personal diagnosis policy through all the grades. Why not? Our physician never stops his diagnostic approach to our physical organisms, he is constantly watching our bodily changes through the passing years, and advising us on that basis. We should be doing so with spiritual interests.

"There's where you will find the explanation of our children dropping out of Sunday-school, mostly in the adolescent years. They face new problems as a result of the awakening of new forces in their organisms and the emergence of new problems in their surroundings, and they need guidance based on as careful diagnosis there. Our teachers lose them from their classes because the teachers do not know how to diagnose and, what is worse, they do not realize any diagnosis is needed. If they did, they would probably try to secure it from someone who has the abilities they lack themselves. Right here in our school, Mr. Alison, we are losing our grip on boys and girls whom I am confident we would stand a good chance to hold, if their teachers only understood better how to watch for evidences of emotional dislocations and, perhaps, bring the cases to you. It is all right to introduce these young people, these high school grade boys and girls to the social problems of the times and the relation of religion to them. By all means let us do that. But at the same time, we must give our first attention to the personality of each one of them and to working out its adjustments.

"I am convinced, too, that this principle should carry right on to us who are adults. Vocational guidance is just as much needed in helping each person to find his proper place in church work as in the work whereby he gets his living."

Alison was deeply impressed with what Martin had brought to him, and frankly told him so. At the same time he reminded him that they would have to go slow in trying to introduce any such radical reorganization; to which Martin readily agreed. Old patterns of work in a church are not readily thrown away. "No man having tasted old wine straightway desireth new, for he saith the old is better!" No, not "straightway"; but in time he will come to relish the new when it shall have shown superior qualities. Alison wanted more time also to consider the new proposal. He was not a man to leap to conclusions and accept a proposal of such importance, no matter how attractive it might appear to be. When the two men parted, it was with the understanding that Martin would give further thought to the working out of details whereby the change in their set-up might be gradually introduced; then they would take it up again.

"Spiritual prophylaxis." The more Alison mused over that term, the more it intrigued him. He had been much immured in spiritual therapy to which he had seen the preventive measures as adjuncts of importance. But spiritual prophylaxis as the *first* responsibility of the church, the "cure" of soul sickness as second; that was quite a reorientation for himself also. Perhaps Martin was right, perhaps we will sometime come to where we shall see such effective spiritual nurtures that there will be less need for the work of restoration. Perhaps we should work with that in view; Alison rather thought we should. However, for the present, we are still surrounded by such great ranks of the spiritually disabled that we must not let up at all on our work of salvage. And just as in medicine it is the study and care of the sick whereby we learn how to preserve the health of those who are still well, so let it be here.

Second Church would continue to put first emphasis on the conserving of spiritual health. As a part of the program, Alison hoped, they would work toward a carefully constructed religious education department with the outlook and ideals Martin had envisioned. If sometime it should come to overshadow that devoted to the reclaiming of the lost by making it less needed, none would rejoice more than he.

VIII

TOWARD WIDER HORIZONS

ALISON'S life at Second Church since the inauguration of the case work program had been a busy one. Of course, he had always been "busy" in the sense that most of the other ministers with whom he associated were. But he had often been dissatisfied over it. So much of what he did seemed to be just puttering around with all sorts of extraneous things. Here he was everlastingly going to meetings. There was a never-ending round of conferences, luncheons, clubs, dinners, and what did it all amount to? Just a repetitious round of talkfests. Reports and resolutions on everything from the race question in the South to the revolutions in China or the proper length of women's dresses. Talk, talk; "everybody talks and nobody does anything" in so many instances. Alison wondered sometimes whether much of it was not because it gave one a chance to make speeches and feel important and then rationalize about concern for public causes and for social progress! And committees and boards! He felt himself almost organized to death. It seemed as though everyone who thought he had a bright idea about something to be done, had to start one more organization and get the ministers on the board.

With the inauguration of his new program of work, Alison proceeded to cut this sort of calendar to the bone. Henceforth he would take on only such things as he could see related to his real job.

It was well that he did so, for that job kept constantly growing as his case load increased from week to week. Happily he was by nature an organizer. Andrew Carnegie had a quaint way of explaining his business success by saying he knew how to surround himself with men who could do the work better than he himself could. Alison had this same skill in picking persons to do work and enlisting their enthusiasm in it. He was constantly tying his people into various parts of the programs he projected in his cases. But with all this there always remained a considerable residuum he had to administer himself. His date book for conferences seemed always full. And yet he always seemed to find time for the emergency calls that came in so frequently.

Much of the work seemed slow and unpromising, but every once in a while some case would break through with a joyous adjustment that seemed in itself ample return for all his strenuous hours of effort. Clinical work was much worthwhile. He was sure of that. So were his people. Every Sunday he seemed to feel himself more closely bound to them. It was because of mutual understanding, he realized that. As he sat in his pulpit and glanced around over his audiences, he met appreciative responses on every side from persons who had unburdened their hearts to him, and with whom he had gone through travail of soul as together they had analyzed a personal problem, searched the inner recesses of motives and wishes and then constructed and carried out programs of adjustment whereby there had come surcease of conflict and joy in living. Work together in these capacities was making Second Church a real fellowship of believers more closely knit together than ever before.

And yet he was not satisfied. They were not yet reaching out as he felt they should to the unchurched people in the neighborhood.

The cause, he decided, was in the matter of making contacts. Merely running in on people to get acquainted and be friendly was not enough. Trying in this way to get them interested in the church was still worse. People are pestered every day by agents for just about everything, till they build up a sales resistance that is an impregnable defense against even an offer of religion. He saw clearly that promotion of the church's enterprise must be undertaken by some other methods than the advertising techniques of commercialism against which the people are now fortified with such effective defense mechanisms.

He set himself to a careful study of the various efforts they had made to extend the church's outreach in the community, comparing successes with failures and looking for causes. As he did so he discovered this fact: that their successes ordinarily came where there had been some keenly felt need in the life of some person or family, perhaps sickness or death, financial loss or other trouble, and where the ministries of the church had been of help. The more he studied this fact, the more its importance grew upon him. Even in cases in which people had been enlisted by giving them tasks to do, the same principle obtained. They had been given an opportunity to gratify a need for worth while self expression.

He became convinced that the whole strategy of attack should be one of finding an instance of need, and helping those involved to find a surcease of suffering or at least an understanding fellowship in enduring it. In so doing there would usually be discovered some spiritual interest involved which religious experience could best conserve, and thereby would come a new understanding and appreciation of religion itself.

But how were these contacts with need to be secured? With his own people that was simple; they understood and sought such contacts. In some cases also they had personal relations with acquaintances whom they guided to the church. Alison himself was active in various community enterprises through which he became known to some of the people. But all this was inadequate. The great majority of the people in the community remained untouched. And he could not but feel that among these were included many who were most spiritually needy. Other ways must be found.

In Hospital Wards

While Alison was still wrestling with this problem he had occasion to make a trip to the nation's capital. While there he by chance came into contact with the program of hospital work carried on by the city's churches through their Federation. It occurred to him that he might perhaps find here at least a partial answer to his question, so he investigated further.

He found a remarkable program of using hospital experience as a means of putting patients in contact with appropriate churches, and thereby not only helping meet the immediate needs of the patients, but in many cases establishing what became enduring church connections for them. There was, for example, a large maternity hospital, the majority of whose patients were young women, many experiencing motherhood for the first time. He was told that more than a thousand such young women had been visited there during the preceding year who were of Protestant antecedents, and more than half of them had no church connections in the city. As the hospital secretary of the Federation made her rounds of visits among these patients, talking with them, seeing that layettes or appropriate little conveniences were provided, and perhaps leaving appropriate leaflets or other literature, she tactfully suggested the readiness of the churches she represented to be of any assistance they could render the patient or her family. Quite commonly on the secretary's second call the patient would detain her for a little chat, in which she would disclose such facts as where she lived, the church to which she naturally felt drawn, and, very often, some circumstance in her situation, perhaps other children at home or a young husband naturally concerned, and indicate some little service she would appreciate. The secretary would then proceed to enlist the interest of the pastor or someone else of that church in the case. While the secretary acknowledged that she had some discouragements in earlier times because of lack of understanding interest on the part of pastors, there was now fine co-operation. Many of the churches had taken on this type of service as a regular part of their organized women's work, with some woman designated as their contact person, whose name was given to the secretary and through whom such cases were reported to that church for such further ministries as the secretary might suggest. A similar set-up had also been effected in other hospitals among patients with various types of disorders.

Alison was thrilled with what he had found. Here was one partial answer to his question. At home they had a Federation of Churches, but he had never heard of anything like this on its program. He decided he would take it up with them at once.

When he did so a little later, he found the executive committee only slightly interested. All were pastors, several of whom began talking about how busy they were and how their many meetings left them little time for calling on the sick outside their own people. One suggested that the city council ought to provide a salary for someone to look after this. Alison thought of his own former little "busy-nesses" from which he had unburdened himself, but he said nothing. The secretary of the Federation recalled that the Salvation Army did have a regular visitor at the City Hospital and he understood she was particularly interested in the maternity ward. The Federation had recently furnished substantial assistance to the Salvation Army in its campaign for funds, and it was felt by the committee that they could secure some such service from the Army's representative for such pastors as were interested. It was decided that this would be undertaken. Soon afterwards the secretary secured the desired order from the Army's headquarters.

When Alison secured a conference with the Army's representative, he found her cooperative but quite evidently surprised. She had so often been disappointed by ministers whom she had tried to enlist in cases, that she had wondered whether she might be wrong in assuming that such things really came within their appointed work. She would certainly be most happy to inform Second Church of any cases from that part of the city in which they might be of help. Incidentally, she revealed the fact that her work extended also into many sections of other hospitals in the city.

The next week Alison received a telephone call from the Army worker. A young man whose home was near the church was in the hospital where he had been critically ill with typhoid. The crisis had passed, but he was very much worried. During his sickness his wife had given birth to their first baby. They had only recently come to the city and were living in a small apartment near Second Church. On top of it all, he had lost his job.

Alison at once took the whole story to Mrs. Allen, wife of one of his elders, who lived near the young people's apartment. When she called there she found that the landlady, a Catholic woman, had been looking after the young mother and child as best she could. The next day Alison called again on the young man in the hospital, assured him that his wife and child were getting along nicely, and told him about Mrs. Allen who would keep in touch with them constantly. During the conversation he learned that the young man was a skilled mechanic in the very line of construction work in which Mr. Allen was engaged. He said nothing at the time, but a few days later when he again called, he told the young man that Mr. Allen was looking for a mechanic with precisely his qualifications and would give him work as soon as he was able to undertake it.

Today that young man has a flourishing business of his own, he and his wife are active members of Second Church, tithers, laying aside one-tenth of their income for religious and charitable work, and participating in all the deeper spiritual activities of the church.

While this young man was still in the hospital Alison one morning found a front page story in his daily paper about a police lieutenant named Rayburn having been hit by an automobile the night before and taken to the hospital seriously injured. The story indicated that there was suspicion that it was not a case of simple accident, since Rayburn was known to have enemies in the underworld. Alison had known the lieutenant, who lived in the Second Church neighborhood, in connection with some law enforcement work a few months before. Alison had been one of a group of citizens who had gone to Rayburn and made complaint against certain vice resorts which were doing a great deal of harm among the young people of the neighborhood. Rayburn had indicated that the resorts had strong political backing, but he would go after them vigorously if the citizens would back him. The ensuing fight had been bitter. When the resort people found they could neither bribe nor frighten nor fool the lieutenant, they undertook to have him removed from the district. It was only after Alison and those associated with him had carried their fight to the public through the pulpit and the press that the resort people were effectively checkmated and Rayburn was retained. Alison also recalled hearing of threats on the part of the resort people that they would "get" Rayburn. He wondered whether this had anything to do with the auto accident. He decided to call on the lieutenant the first time he visited the hospital.

When he did so, he found the situation much more serious than he had anticipated. Rayburn had been run over and suffered a crushed hip and broken pelvis. He was suffering intensely, as he continued to do for several weeks. He knew that he would come out of the hospital a cripple, lamed for life. During all this time Alison was a frequent visitor. Rayburn had never manifested any interest in religion. On the other hand, he had rather indicated that it was of little concern to real men, and he had accepted Alison in spite of his being a minister rather than because of it. As these visits continued during his long illness, however, he began to see it in a different light. Alison was understandingly sympathetic without anything maudlin in his attitudes. What he contributed most was the impact of his own personality. It was that of one brave man on another brave man. He did not at once presume to offer prayer there in the midst of the busy nurses, but he did manage to refer quietly to help from God and say in parting, "I will be praying for you." Rayburn pressed his hand in a way that Alison understood.

As soon as Rayburn was sufficiently recovered to be able to talk connectedly he told him quite freely about the whole occurrence. It was evident that he felt this was one man to whom he could do so. The auto had been driven by a woman who had conducted one of the worst of the resorts he had raided and closed. Of course, she had witnesses to prove that her running over the lieutenant was purely accidental, indeed, they were ready to testify that it was in no sense her fault but really entirely his own because he had stepped right in front of her machine so that she could not avoid striking him. The fact that they all happened to be just there at that time was to say the least quite remarkable, but they would no doubt have ready explanation for that also.

Alison understood. Here was a casualty in a war for which he was himself partly responsible. He realized he was gazing into the eyes of a brave man who had unflinchingly done his duty, and who was now as unflinchingly having no regrets for having done so.

And yet, deep in those eyes Alison saw a question. Why all this? If there is a good God in Heaven, why should one suffer thus for trying to stop the exploitation of the weak and unwary, while the exploiter continues to ride about in comfort? Rayburn had never before given much thought to such things. He did not know much about religion, less about philosophy.

But he believed in Alison.

In the days that followed, the two virile men talked much with each other. Alison prayed with Rayburn. For they had come to where Rayburn asked him to do so. They faced life's mystery together.

And Rayburn saw it through.

He is now an elder in Second Church. He looks back on those hospital days as the end of his police career, but the beginning of his Christian career. They were days when he saw his life ambitions crushed with his crushed hip. But they were days when he found new meanings in life, new aims in life, new values in life which moth and rust cannot corrupt and which even the cruising automobile of a resort owner cannot run down and destroy. He does not blame God for his injury, but he does thank God for the counsel and fellowship given him in those cruel days by one who had helped save him from cynicism, pessimism and despair.

With the passing of time Alison found his work at the hospital, and that of his people who were enlisted in it, constantly growing in the appreciation of doctors and others of the hospital staff. Much of what they did was akin to the work of the social agencies, but in many cases the easement needed by a patient concerning a home situation, for example, is something that can be more acceptably done by a neighbor introduced through a church where there is no professional service involved. Their outstanding contribution, however, was of course in religion itself and what it afforded to the emotional state of the sufferer. Ordinarily this was in the form of hope rekindled and rest afforded by the establishment of faith. Hope without faith is dead. Indeed, it never rises. Faith in the doctor, faith in science, faith in one's own recuperative powers, all of these are mightily strengthened when they can be undergirded by a philosophy of life with a loving God back of it all and a confidence in one's own fellowship with Him.

But Alison's program envisioned more than just the immediate easement of a patient's suffering, important as he realized that to be. And it included more also than the spiritual ministrations to those about to die. After all, more than ninety per cent of these people in the hospitals are going to return to their homes, the majority of them to recover sufficiently to enter again the swirl of things which had formerly absorbed most of their attention, and in many instances left little apparent opportunity for attention to things spiritual. He was concerned that their meditations in these days of enforced mental leisure should be of a kind that would not only further their return to health but would also carry over into spiritual wholesomeness in the years to follow.

> "When the Devil was sick, the Devil a saint would be;
> But when the Devil got well, the Devil a saint was he!"

Alison wanted always to be safeguarded against promoting no better religion than that. That was the reason for his high appreciation of the policies he found in Washington, as over against the traditional one of providing a hospital chaplain whose attentions ordinarily end with the patient's discharge from the institution. He was concerned about provisions being made which would establish or strengthen church ties the sustaining values of which would continue to obtain through the succeeding years.

Working With the Courts

Alison was one day at lunch with two other ministers. They had been discussing local civic conditions, some unquestionably unwholesome, and the political factors involved, deploring the prevalence in office of mediocre men or worse, and the way voters generally seem to take so little intelligent interest in political affairs, leaving them to professional politicians. They had just come from a ministers' meeting where a speaker had pleaded with the ministers to take a more active part in promoting a conscientious and intelligent use of the ballot by the people under their influence. Then one of the two ministers, a relatively young man, said:

"I tell you I'm not going to get myself mixed up in politics or anything related to it. Not me! I'm going to be careful. Just last week I had a man and his wife come to see me about their twelve year old boy who had been arrested. It seems some woman had him turned in on a charge of indecent exposure or something like that. They wanted me to go down to the police station and get him out. I didn't let them get me mixed up in anything like that. They were not members of my church anyhow; don't even go to any church. Their boy has been coming to our Sunday-school now and then. I had seen him there. I don't think he had meant anything really bad, because I'm pretty sure he is feeble-minded. But I kept myself clear. I sent them over to see Jim Moran and let him take care of them."

Alison was disgusted. Ordinarily quite self-controlled, this time he cut loose with a vengeance.

"You are the type of fellow that makes me tired! That was about the most stupid thing you ever did! More than that, it was cowardly and abominably selfish!

"You had a rare opportunity to be of real service to those people, and perhaps win a whole family for Christ and the church. Instead of that, you turned them over to a shoestring politician who didn't do them a bit of lasting good, but who will use this to get control of their votes! All he would do would be to call up the desk sergeant and tell him to let the boy go. Then he would be sure that the parents knew that it was his influence that got the boy off. Of course they are going to vote the way that politician wants them to at the next election.

"Why shouldn't they? You would if you were in their place. Talk about "buying" votes! These politicians don't have to "buy" votes like that. All they need to do is wait for men like you to throw them into their hands. They get votes all the time by doing things for people in trouble that you ought to be doing for them. Then you come around here whining about the way people let politicians run the city! Its men just like you who are responsible for the gang you heard about being in control of the city just now!

"And that's not the worst of it. You missed an opportunity to help that family. What you should have done was to go down to the police station with that man and sign the bond for his boy to be released in your care till the hearing the next morning. He wasn't going to run away, his parents would be taking care of him. Then in the morning you should have gone with them to the hearing. You should have told the magistrate what you just told us; that you think the boy is feeble-minded. Then if you had suggested it, the magistrate would have continued the case till the city psychiatrist could look into it. In that way you would have done something constructive for the family for which they would have been always grateful. Probably out of it all you would have won them all for the church.

"You say they do not go to any church. You sure did a lot to encourage them to begin!"

Later in the day as Alison sat musing over the incident, he realized that he himself had no systematized contact with the police courts. He was in the habit of going into them with his cases, but he had no method of meeting people there whom the church might help in their troubles. Why should they not set up something like they were undertaking in the hospitals? He decided to look into the matter.

What he discovered surprised him. In the first

place, he found the police court is the most extensive court in the city, its dockets running anywhere from five to twenty times as many cases as reach the higher courts. It is also the poor man's court, where his troubles with the law begin and where most of them end because he does not have resources to carry them higher. It is the court of the foreigner, where he has his first and ordinarily his only contact with American justice, and naturally judges it by what he experiences there. It is the court of youth, particularly those of later adolescent years who constitute by far the largest part of the persons brought into it. It is the court where family disturbances emerge, where the victim of drink is brought, where the erring girl faces her accusers, where the first offender first faces the cost of crime. Unfortunately, it is a court too often manned with political appointees with no social training, little social vision, low spiritual ideals, men who are blatantly cynical, pessimistic, sophisticated.

What tragedies must go on there constantly!

What an opportunity for Christian service of the highest order!

Inasmuch as the largest proportion of cases involved later adolescent boys, Alison decided to go to the Y.M.C.A. about it. There he found an understanding interest at once. Shortly afterwards the matter was taken up with the Federation of Churches and a cooperative program was formed.

The Y.M.C.A. agreed to furnish a secretary to attend the court hearings, and the court arranged for him to have a desk in an appropriate room where interviews could be held. The Federation agreed to act as an agency furnishing connection with the churches so they could help carry out programs in connection with cases as they developed. It was understood that the secretary would be able in many cases to render direct service, particularly in the cases of boys, but it was made quite plain that he was not to think of his duties as ending there. Of equal importance was his making contacts with the boy's own church or sort some other appropriate one for a longer follow-up and a wider service than he could render. While his own personal services would be primarily with boys in the court, it was agreed that for the time being he would act as a clearing agent also for other cases in which the services of the churches could be used.

The authorities at the court were entirely cooperative, though they showed themselves somewhat skeptical about the preachers doing anything very much worthwhile. The secretary sent by the Y.M.C.A. was more doubtful on this point himself than he would openly admit. But he was satisfied Alison at least would play the game intelligently. He would use Alison.

The Mavic Family

Alison's first case from the court came within a few days. A Czechoslovac girl of seventeen had been arrested for stealing a blouse from a department store. The court was holding the case over for further investigation and the store representative had talked with the Y.M.C.A. secretary about it, who suggested that Alison be asked to cooperate. One of the Second Church women who lived near the girl's home called on the family. She found them in abject poverty. They had come to America some eight years before. They were from the land of John Huss and looked forward to great opportunities in famed America. Two years ago, the father had died, broken in heart and health by prolonged idleness during depression times. Recently the oldest son on whose small income the family chiefly depended, had become discouraged and had run away and joined the army. The family now consisted of the arrested girl, a sister aged twelve and a younger brother who was a cripple confined to bed. The whole family lived in one room facing an alley, and was entirely without income. The accused girl had been working in a restaurant and keeping the family since the brother ran away, but had recently been discharged for lying and suspected stealing.

A policewoman who had also been assigned to the case, and who was working in cooperation with the church, decided it would be best to send the girl to an institution for a time, the Second Church agreeing to look after the family. The first thing to do was to secure temporary financial aid from the Welfare Department and to move the family into a healthful two-room apartment. A position was secured for the woman at the Goodwill Industries. Through the local health center a brace was secured for the crippled boy, and treatment undertaken whereby within two years he was able to go about and had become almost a normally healthy boy.

In the meantime the family had become connected with Second Church. Their background in their homeland had been Protestant, but they had no church connections in America. The younger daughter entered high school where she learned stenography. The older girl continued in the institution to which she was committed for about a year. During that time Second Church people kept in touch with her as well as with her family. She came back an earnest Christian and a year later was happily married. Recently she said to the Second Church woman who had kept in touch with the family throughout, "I thank God for what you people have done for me and my family. It saved them and has made a woman of me!"

From the police court connections Alison soon found himself dealing also with the probation service and later with the parole office also. A friend had told him of a set-up in Indianapolis where connections had been established through a Federation of churches whereby practically all probation cases were introduced to appropriate churches for cooperation with probation officers in restoration work. Alison realized it would not be possible at this time to get anything of that kind established here, so he decided he would try to work himself with the local offices, at least on cases with which they had been given initial contact in the police court. He found the probation officers more than willing to cooperate and most appreciative of what the church could do to help them, burdened as they were with case loads far in excess of what could be carried adequately.

At the same time he sensed at times an undertone of uncertainty, as though there was doubt about how far the churches would go in staying with cases given to their care. One day when he was in the probation office, one of the officers showed him a report of a conference he had attended the preceding year in Albany. In it was an address made by a woman who had been in parole service for many years and who was herself an actively religious person, one indeed the officer said, who had just recently left that service to enter a religious order. Alison secured permission to copy portions of that address which he took down as follows:

"I have been in the office of the Division of Parole almost from the beginning. On various occasions we have tried getting some official cooperation from religious groups in the city. None of them cooperated with any clear-cut and definite responsibility to help us with a religious program. We then tried it on the basis of a case work plan, working from the individual case. We tried, for example, to have the pastor of the church or temple of which the parolee or his family was a member, to take hold of the problem. We tried to secure the interest of some representative clergymen to help the parolees. I must say, however, of all the religious groups without exception, that the clergymen have not been interested in helping parolees, that they have been definitely uninterested.

"We then tried to interest the religious groups before the men came out on parole. For a period of several months we absolutely required the parole officers while making their preparole investigations, to establish a contact wth the priest or minister or rabbi who would have a natural interest in that parolee when he came out. That experience resulted in the fact that, when we approached clergymen of all the different groups, the response was, 'What do you want me to do? What can I do?'

"There was very little grasp of what could be done for the individual parolee in any of these groups. After spending a great deal of time in doing that and getting no practical results, we gave up making it an absolute requirement, and have gotten down to where we find that some parole officers do succeed in interesting a few clergymen in their territory to taken an interest. But we totally fail in getting any mass cooperation from the religious groups with any plan on their part to help us with an organized system."

It was because of experiences such as these, then, that the men in his office were somewhat skepical about what was to be expected from the ministers. Alison felt stung by the truth in the charges of this Christian woman.

At the same time he realized that this situation did not obtain because his brethren of the ministry were callous and unconcerned. It was because they did not know how. They had never been trained for such personal service, never even been given to understand it was a part of their professional work. Of course they frequently read to their people from the sayings of Jesus, "I was in prison and ye visited me," but it seemed to have meant nothing more to them than the exact meaning of that English word, "visited." Of course they were ready to do that. They would not hesitate to visit. They would go and "preach to the spirits in prison." But further than that they knew not what to do.

Until there was a better preparation of ministers in their training, until there was a better organized system in their churches to carry forward programs of case work, Alison saw little prospect of the Indianapolis plan getting far here. In the meantime, however, Second Church would do what it could. Help the probation and parole officers? Yes, but he was not thinking in those terms. He was thinking of the probationer and the parolee and of their families, and he was thinking of the spiritual ministries needed in their circumstances, ministries of a kind which officers of the law should not be expected to furnish, but which are the distinctive contribution to be sought from religious agencies. Quite as often as not, these ministries needed to be made even more to others in the home situation than just to the offender now in the hands of the law, others whom the skilled case worker quickly saw were largely responsible for situations which had contributed in large measure to the downfall of the one now in trouble. It was not to be expected that the officer could do much for these. But here was the larger opportunity of the Church.

Wider horizons: Alison had looked upon them that historic morning when he stood bewildered in the vestibule of Second Church. Now he was looking down new avenues of approach toward them which had been opened by Second Church, and along which progress was being made.

He found in it a new encouragement and a new confidence.

IX

PARISH CASE WORK IN PROCESS

WHAT should be the church's policy in the way of making records of its cases?

Alison found this to be one of his most baffling problems. On the one hand it was the universal policy of all standard social agencies. Without exception they consider adequate records essential to good case work. Faithfulness and skill in this is one of the most important standards by which they appraise their own work. And ability in case recording receives an emphasis second to nothing else in the training of a social worker. On the other hand was the all but universal practice of the churches to keep no such personal records whatever. More than that, it was unquestionably the prevailing sentiment among church people that it would be highly improper to do so. Did not the Bible explicitly say, "Let not thy left hand know what they right hand doeth?" Then there is the danger that curious eyes may scan these records, and what scandals they might produce! It is hard enough at the best to live down one's wrong doings and misfortunes without having the church itself keep their record all down in black and white. Christian churches ought to be Christian enough themselves to do for the unfortunates what every one of us wants God to do for him, that is to "blot out all our transgressions from the book of thy remembrance and remember them no more against us forever!"

It was not an easy question, not by any means one-sided; Alison realized that. Moreover, he knew that ministers are utterly untrained in the technique of case recording and know little more about its use and interpretation. He remembered what had happened to very meagre membership records which he had kept in his former parish and turned over to his successor in that pastorate. A few months later he was called up on the telephone by this succeeding pastor and asked for some information about certain members. Alison said to him that he would find all that on the record cards he had given him. "Oh, those cards," the man said; "I threw them all into the waste basket long ago!" Such was the fate of several years faithful recording, when it got into the hands of a really good man whose training and experience had given him no idea whatever of its value.

Nevertheless Alison saw clearly that records of some kind would be absolutely necessary if effective case work was to be done. They would at least be available as long as the present pastorate continued. And it might be hoped that by that time the people themselves would have come to understand their value enough to see that they were not destroyed.

On the other hand, it was just as important that these records be kept absolutely confidential. It would never do to have them available to be read by the people of the church in general, not even by those who might be helping on a case in which they were helping to make the record. That was one regard in which case recording in a church must differ decidedly from that of a social agency, such as a family welfare society, whose records are open to all workers connected with the agency. It was therefore decided that these records, while they would be kept in a folder system similar to those of the social agencies, nevertheless would be kept in a locked file accessible only to the minister and his assistant or secretary. To afford further safeguard for the personal confidences some of these records might contain, it was also decided to use a system of symbols and pseudonyms whereby the actual names and much of the identifying materials would not appear on the face of the records. A key to the interpretation of these would be known only to the minister and his assistant. Something of this kind was necessary in order to insure safeguards similar to those the physician has provided for himself in the use of technical medical terms and symbols which the layman cannot understand. The sanctity of personal confidences must be guarded here as elsewhere.

But all these safeguards could obtain, and still records could be kept, such as would be necessary if cases were to be carried over periods of years. And as time went on, some Second Church cases were certain to become long-term ones. Increasing experience alone could determine what materials should go into these records and in what forms. There were no adequate precedents in all this for Second Church to follow. It had to make its own.

The Casey Family

The Casey family was an example of a long-time case where records of some kind were essential.

This problem came to Alison's hands when Mr. Casey was arrested for larceny of some goods which he admitted taking from his employers. The firm was loath to press the prosecution, so it had been referred at their request to the probation office for further investigation. The officer learned there was some connection of the family with Second Church so he had come to Alison with the case. The church had by this time provided Alison with an assistant, a mature woman of some experience and training in social work. He already knew something about the Caseys, but his assistant was set to work at getting the whole setting of the case. She brought the following story to him as the basis for their records:

Mrs. Casey, a woman of thirty-five, had long been affiliated with Second Church. She came of a Scotch-Irish family of sterling character and financial integrity. The father died shortly after the family came to America. The others, by dint of hard work, careful economy and remarkable family cooperation, had managed to maintain a good home and give all the children a high school education. All of them had been successful or fortunate in their business, professional and marital relations except Mrs. Casey. One of her sisters married a missionary, another a minister, a third married a successful business man who, with her, is an active member of Second Church.

There were two brothers; one is a minister, the other a successful business man.

Mr. Casey is from an old New England family, Protestant, but none of his family was particularly interested in religion. So far as known, they are thrifty and honest, one of his brothers holding a position of trust in a large corporation.

Upon graduation from high school Mr. Casey secured a position with a wholesale dry-goods firm. There, after a few years, he met Mrs. Casey who was a stenographer in the office. He advanced rapidly with the company and began attending Second Church with her. Eventually they were married with the full approval of both families, though some of his people "guyed" him somewhat over marrying such a religious girl. Their early married life was quite happy. Both were busy and active in Second Church. She was a choir singer and teacher in the church school, he was an usher and at one time served as president of the Men's Brotherhood. Later he was made treasurer of the church.

A few years after their marriage he went into business for himself, a retail dry-goods business, taking a friend as a silent partner, who invested a thousand dollars in the enterprise. They expanded the business rapidly and soon had three stores in different parts of the city with flourishing trade in all of them. Then labor troubles in the largest mill in their part of the city over a prolonged period brought on a local depression, as a result of which two of the three stores failed. The other, however, seemed to be flourishing.

Casey also developed a brokerage business in woolens which he sold to other stores in large cities.

After a time he became careless in his book accounts, confusing those of the store and the brokerage business and the funds of the church, providing no definite salary for himself but drawing money from the business at will for personal uses. Then the accuracy of his accounts with the church had been challenged. He had no adequate book accounts, and left that office under a cloud of suspicion.

Not long after that the banks began to close down on his business, and he proceeded to borrow money from family and friends, becoming very unreliable in repayment. Finally he closed the dry-goods business, giving his creditors notes none of which has ever been paid. He then took a position as a salesman for a Jewish firm of credit clothiers and proved himself a superior salesman. His wages were fifty dollars a week. However, he got behind in his accounts with his employers and finally was discharged. Shortly after that he secured a similar position with another firm in the same line of business at a slightly higher salary. Of this he gave his wife twenty dollars a week, apparently spending the rest rather freely. The firm put him in charge of a branch store with a drawing account of two hundred and fifty dollars. Recently on checking his stock, they found fifty garments missing for which there were no sales slips. A detective found three of these suits being worn by members of his family, to whom he had given them saying he had paid for them, which was not true. This was followed by his arrest. He has admitted taking the goods and using the drawing account for his own purposes and has signed a statement to that effect.

Personally, Casey is a good-natured affable sort of person, kind to his wife and children, an effective salesman with an unusually persuasive manner. Around the home he is cooperative, interested in the good behavior of his children. On the other hand he is unsystematic, lacks steadiness of purpose, begins a new enterprise with enthusiasm, then soon neglects it and fails to carry it through.

The probation officer had been to see Mrs. Casey. She begged for a chance to work for the money herself wherewith to repay the firm and thus save the family honor. She had taken a position in a department store and supported the family for a time, he drifting about at odd jobs and accomplishing nothing. He is now entirely out of work and she is reported ill.

Alison's assistant had just come from a call at the Casey home. She found Mrs. Casey in a state of emotional unbalance bordering on hysteria. She had been suffering from a seriously infected sore throat which the doctor says is complicated by her anxieties and worries. The family is also almost without resources. It consists of a daughter of fourteen and two younger brothers. Mrs. Casey is reported to have said recently that she intends securing a legal separation from her husband and breaking up the home.

When this report was brought in, Alison and his assistant studied it long and carefully. Alison now understood something of why he had never been able to get near to the Casey family or learn much about them. Casey himself had never come about the church since Alison became pastor, and had seemed to shun him. Mrs. Casey also attended but rarely.

Manifestly here was anything but a simple problem, involving several people.

There was first of all, Casey himself. It was evident that personality problems were involved, possibly such as would need the aid of a psychiatrist. Here were strange inconsistencies which might betoken serious mental illness. They might, however, be the effects of conflicts between the idealisms and the moral standards of his earlier background on the one side, and the different idealisms and attitudes of his wife and her family, with whom he is now associated and to whom he is undoubtedly bound by affectional ties. If the first should be the case, institutional care would probably be necessary. If the second obtains, then the task comes back to the church.

Then there was Mrs. Casey, now in a disturbed condition that might easily become precarious. And there were the three children and all the rest of her closely-knitted family, with its cherished social standing and reputation for integrity. No course could be taken regarding any of these people that would not affect them all.

It seemed quite evident that the place to begin was with Mrs. Casey, and that Alison was the one to undertake it. She knew him and presumably had full confidence in him, and her whole history was of a kind that should make it easiest for her to unburden herself to a minister of her own church. Alison called to see her that afternoon.

He found her wrapped up in a reclining chair by the fireside. She welcomed him, and yet there was a strained anxiety in her manner that revealed at once her shame over what she felt was a family disgrace, and her wonder as to how much Alison knew about it and what he thought of it all. The younger son was in the room busy with his home work from school.

Alison's manner was cordial, cheerful but not too much so, as though he knew there was a "situation" and understood. There was something about his air that made Mrs. Casey feel that he not only knew, but that he understood the situation perhaps better than she did and might be able to suggest what to do. He began with inquiry about her health, and talked about that kind of an infection in a chatty sort of way that released her from much of her tenseness. He then turned to the boy, talked a little to him about his school work and managed to get in a suggestion about something else to be done, which the mother quickly took up and thus found an excuse for having the boy leave the room. Alison was now alone with her so that she could talk freely.

He at once introduced the subject which each of them knew they were both thinking about. So he did it quite frankly. But he did it in a way that carried no sense of shock, no suggestion of blame, only manifest understanding. "I'm glad of this chance to have a few words with you alone, Mrs. Casey, so that we can talk over these troubles that are now embarrassing Mr. Casey and, of course, the rest of you too. I fancy he is going to depend a great deal on you, for I know how fond he is of you and how much he esteems your counsel."

That was a good lead. Its naturalness still more released her tenseness, its respectful reference to Casey relieved her from revealing either excuse or condemnation for him, and the reference to his affection and esteem for her relieved her from any sense of helplessness.

"It is terrible!" she ventured.

"I would hardly put it that way," he replied. "Of course it is unfortunate, and we are going to have something of a job finding what to do about it. But you know there is a lot of good stuff in Mr. Casey, and you are fortunate in having such a good standing in the community yourself and so many friends. I am sure we will find a way to adjust things. Please tell me everything I ought to know about it."

That last phrase appealed to her; "everything I ought to know." That means he is not here to pry but to learn how he can be of help. Here was a man she could trust.

Despite her sore throat, she started and poured out her very soul to him; all the shame and chagrin of this awful exposure; the long years of reckless handling of money on Casey's part, which her Scotch-Irish thrift ranked as little less than mortal sin; the disgrace of his treasurer's account in the church never having been cleared up; his lack of deep concern over it all;

his slip-shod way of working on other jobs secured for him so that he soon lost them all; his apparently nonchalant unconcern over his disgrace and that of his family; most of all his seeming lack of any sense of sin, which her own Christian background made her feel most deeply of all. At times she became somewhat hysterical, particularly when something turned her thoughts back to the happier days of her courtship and earlier married life. But Alison's understanding manner and calm self control helped her quickly to re-establish her own.

What was she to do now?

That was the question that concerned her most, at least in her conscious thinking. She could not go on living with him as things are now. The disgrace of it all and his seeming unconcern would make her loathe his presence. But how could she divorce him? That would be further disgrace! And her family; her children; her so-highly respected brothers and sisters, how could she ever face them! Then of course there was the financial need. If only she were well, she would work somewhere to support the family. But how could she make enough to pay off his debts also? The outlook seemed only dark. If she could only die! But that would make matters worse, for then who would care for the children and pay the debt? No, she must not die. She must get well and somehow carry on!

Alison let her run on with her recital, interrupting once in awhile with a directing question only. To rest her aching throat, he now broke in with some conversation of no particular import to keep her quiet while she eased the pain with sips of water. Bad as the strain of talking was, he knew that this would be more than compensated by the nerve release and the relaxation which would follow. When he felt that she had told enough to relieve her heart and to give him ground on which to start to build, he took the conversation from her. Saying he realized her throat must now be getting tired, he began his reply.

She settled back to listen.

He did not tell her much about what was to be done. What he did do was make it plain that he did not consider the situation nearly as bad as she feared, and that he had no doubt the whole situation could be cleared up so that all would be relieved. They would not forget that after all they had their Christian faith, and this was a time for them to let it have free course and demonstrate its value. They would remember that God loves and cares, and they can still say, "So long thy hand hath led me, sure it still will lead me on!" They would go farther and try to say in assured faith, "I do not ask to see the distant scene, one step enough for me!"

That next step, he believed, was to try to think this all through and wait for God's guidance. In the meantime it was her job to get back her poise by a resurgence of her faith. That also would help bring back her health.

About Casey? Alison was frank to say he did not yet know. He wanted to talk with him, to learn more about him, to study him more closely. In the meantime he would see that some adjustment was made to meet the court issue for the present, and thus prevent further embarrassment to the family while things were being worked out.

When he left, Mrs. Casey was quiet and evidently much relieved.

The next step, of course, was to interview Casey. There was no difficulty in securing an appointment. When invited to talk things over with the pastor he readily did so. At first he was jauntily careless, evidently assuming that it would be easy to fool the preacher. But Alison's manner soon showed him that he was not accomplishing that. At the same time it was a courteous and understanding attitude that made it impossible to take offense. As the conversation went on and it became more and more evident that the minister both knew what he was talking about and what Casey was trying to do, and yet treated him respectfully as a man, Casey found himself more and more warming up to the pastor. Yes, he came really to like him, what was more, to trust him.

And yet he could not bring himself to uncover. He kept himself concealed behind a store-front mask which he realized Alison knew was a mask. He really wanted to reveal his real self, and again and again seemed to be setting out to do so, then would suddenly shy off into unessentials. He did not any longer conceal the fact that there was something back of his troubles which he had not yet uncovered. But Alison was pretty sure Casey himself did not know what it was. When Casey had been saying to his wife and others that he did not know why he did as he did, he was probably telling the truth. Alison was not at all sure there was not some serious mental disturbance, and decided it would be most desirable to have a psychiatrist brought into touch with him. That would clear the atmosphere and let Alison know more of what he should himself undertake. When they parted, it was with the understanding that Alison would try to get the probation period extended by the courts while plans were being worked out to make some kind of an adjustment of his financial shortages, and that the two of them would be conferring from time to time over the whole situation.

Several weeks went by, during which, at Alison's suggestion, the court saw to it that Casey was gone over quite carefully by the court psychiatrist. He reported that the man was in no sense insane, there was no psychosis of any kind. He was emotionally unstable, probably because of some conflicts which had not been disclosed. These might inhere in his affectional relations to his family and others, or they might be in the realm of his system of life values, his idealisms.

Alison began to wonder whether these conflicts might not be in the religious area. Casey had grown up in an atmosphere of superciliousness toward religion as something not to be taken seriously. Then he had fallen deeply in love with his wife and had accepted her religion as a part of her. In a sense, she was his religion. God had come into his mental content, but it was just as a piece of mental furniture, given place there because his wife thought it ought to be there, much as he approved of that piece of antique furniture beside the mantlepiece in the parlor because his wife thought it should be there. He now defended religion among his old associates just as he defended anything else his wife thought valuable. He enjoyed the fellowships of the church people and honestly tried to conform to their ideals because they were not much different from the ones he already had. They were indeed about the same, except for this important difference; they rested on different bases. With him, they were good ideals because they were promising ones. "Honesty is the best policy," therefore be honest. So with the others. The religious viewpoint, in which ideals receive their sanction in a conviction that they inhere in the character of God and that life's worthwhileness inheres finally in fellowship with God, was something he simply had never sensed at all.

If this were the case, then Casey's delinquencies would begin to be understandable. They probably came because his moral foundations were insecure and his frequent instabilities, fluctuations and frivolities were forms of escape from the deeper demands of a soul that had not yet found God. If that were the case too, religion and religion alone could make a man of him.

But to accomplish this would take a religious experience reaching down into depths of his being which had never yet been sounded. That was not to be accomplished quickly. Very likely it could come only after he had suffered deeply. He had not yet done so. Indeed, every indication was that Casey had never allowed himself to suffer much over anything. Even the present trouble he had succeeded in keeping on the surface levels only of his emotional life. This he did by means of his superficial ethics. "Christ bought the keys of paradise by cruel bleeding." No man ever rises to any great spiritual heights, nor does one ever fathom spiritual depths except at the cost of suffering, Alison knew that well. Perhaps the present sufferings of Casey's wife might help. It was evident they were hard for Casey to throw off. For unquestionably he loved her deeply. Perhaps he would himself be brought to suffer by the sight of her suffering with the consciousness that he had caused it. Was it possible that by her sufferings he might be saved? If it might be so, she would gladly endure it for his salvation. Alison would wait and watch. Somehow Casey must be helped to sound deeper levels.

In the meantime there was Mrs. Casey and the rest of the family.

The court case was quietly adjusted through the probation office so that the defaulted money could be paid back in installments. Thus the children were saved from embarrassment, and at Alison's suggestion their mother never discussed it in their presence.

But that only made it all the more imperative that there be some other to whom she might unburden her soul. That, of course, was Alison. Gently he led her to more hopeful thoughts about her husband, though being careful not to arouse expectations that might be blasted. One day she said to him, "I have been thinking much about that story you once told about an Aunt Josephine. I am trying to be like her. And I am becoming more confident that our case will work out that way."

The story had been about an acquaintance of Alison in his boyhood. It was a woman who was earnest Christian but whose husband was not. Outwardly he seemed hardened against all religious appeal, but she continued her quiet way, apparently unconcerned. When people spoke to her about it she would rather cheerily reply, "Oh, Port will come some day!" She had put it all in God's hands, and her faith was such that she did not doubt. A day came when her faith was rewarded. "Port," as she called him, went through a deep religious experience from which he continued in nearly twenty years of victorious Christian living. Mrs. Casey came into a faith like that.

With the growth of that faith, Alison saw her find new adjustments in life and restored health.

Alison and Casey have had many talks together but never yet has Casey succeeded in removing the mask. And because he has not sounded deeply enough, he cannot rise to the tablelands of God. But Alison believes he is on his way. The conflict still rages in his soul, probably because there is a second nucleating center of life values held over from his earlier training, in addition to the Christ center he honestly accepted with his wife's religion. Thus with divided fealties, some of his basic impulses attached to one and others to the other, he is literally the scriptural "double minded man, unstable in all his ways."

The problem of what shall be the method of case recording in church work is yet unsolved, so Alison is holding much in the Casey record in the form of symbols which he alone can interpret. Only the essentials which are unembarrassing are plainly set forth, pending such further experience as will indicate more about the form these records should take. But one thing is certain, some such records are indispensable. When it is recalled that Alison has been dealing with the Caseys now for some years and will continue to do so, as will others, and that Casey himself may yet break mentally, it is evident there must be the keeping of record if intelligent follow-up work is to be done.

X

SABBATICAL SUMMARIES

SEVEN years had passed since that Monday morning, historic in Alison's ministry. Again he sat musing in his study. It was the same room, the church building had been little changed, but how little else was the same!

He could well afford to take time from things of the moment to look back over it all, to try to see the succeeding events in this longer perspective. Israel had a practice of seventh year appraisals and readjustments. He could well follow, at least so far as the first of these.

Seven years! How short the span as he recalled the musings of that morning! But how long, as he began to recount all that had intervened! And how different the stage picture, though the setting was the same! How different the *dramatis personæ!*

Different persons? Indeed they were! He was still the pastor and answered to the same name, but what a different pastor he had become! His people likewise, in large part, were those with whose cooperation he began, but they too, how they had changed!

What a different church picture! Changes so radical but so gradually and naturally achieved that it was only in taking this longer view as he was doing this morning, that one could realize how great the changes had been. "The former things are passed away, Behold I make all things new!"

"New?" At least he was a new Alison, he realized that. "Bewildered" was the word that described him then, but not today. The years between have clarified his vision of his work and its meaning. There is no longer any question as to what they are trying to accomplish and the general features of the program to be followed. But there had come changes in himself more profound than that. His own emotional attitudes have changed; he is more patient, more understanding, more mellowed, and, perhaps as a result, more stabilized, more happy.

And those who have gone with him through the travail of these years? He sees like changes in them. Perhaps that is only a projection he is making of his own experiences onto them? He recalled a word of counsel from one of the lectures of his university days which he had written down at the time: "Our judgments of others are projections of ourselves!" Yes, it was no doubt true. But that very projection enabled him to understand more clearly how the changes had proceeded in them, particularly what were the radical changes required in the thinking of many an earnest soul, who for that reason had been longer in the process. He saw now that not a little of the best case work of the period had consisted in the constructive changes brought about in the workers themselves, as they came to know their real selves in the processes of their participation in the analysis of others.

"Our judgments of others are projections of ourselves!"

This morning that sentence kept looming up again and again as a sort of magic key for the interpretation of many of the situations in these seven years over which his mind was now roaming. As one after another, situations which at the time were baffling, developments that had been unexpected, arrested his attention and he now tried to understand them in this longer perspective, this sentence was to the fore in producing his present better understanding.

How revealing was that sentence! It certainly obtains, as the professor had pointed out, whenever one attempts to attribute motives to another or to find ultimate causes of behavior. I can never really perceive why you do what you do, I can only judge what I would consider to be the reason for my doing so if I were in your place. I can never get out of myself into yourself, even in imagination. I can only imagine myself slightly modified by the very few things I do know about you and then acting in your position. It is not the real "you" on which I pass judgment, it is my own idea of you which I have constructed, and into which has entered the really little about you which I know, no matter how intimate our association, and a great deal more of my own ideation which is actually a product of my own individuality and experience. Thus my judgments of others reveal much more about myself than about them.

"Our judgments of others are projections of ourselves!" What light that threw on the controversies in some of their case conferences!

There was that case of a middle-teen aged girl who had been caught picking up things in a five-and-ten-cent store, and the wide difference of opinion concerning her. Mrs. Tinker was sure it was just a thoughtless little whim and felt that when the girl understood she would never do it again. But then, everybody knew Mrs. Tinker, thoroughly good soul, rather simple-minded, brought up in a good home and fortunately married, naively ignorant of the mad pulls of life in its fiercer relations; of course, she thought that way about the girl. It was what would be true of Mrs. Tinker. There was another woman who thought the girl should be treated leniently, but for another reason. She called attention to the fact that all the things taken were what the girl would consider pretty things—jewelry, cosmetic make-ups, petty finery. But this woman was always notable for her fastidious dress and manifest satisfaction in good appearance. Mr. Wood called attention to the fact that the girl's people had a very limited income and there was a large family. He was sure the girl intended no wrong, and should be, at most, lightly punished, because it came from the financial stress of her economic need. But Mr. Wood was himself a man with small income and a large family and was a socialist. Marian Freeling had no patience with the girl, was sure she was just a bad girl, as a lot of worthless girls of the working class are, and ought to be taught her place. She was probably trying to show herself off and appear like girls not of her class. Probably she was just one more of those girls who never work if they can help it, don't want to work and always want others to support them. Mr. Wood, however, nearly started something when he broke in to say that he fully agreed with Miss Freeling, that we would all be better off without girls who never work, don't intend to work, and are depending on others who do work to support them. Then he mentioned the wealthiest heiress in town and suggested we begin with her! Marian's finely manicured hands twitched and Alison noticed that she covered her two diamond rings. But she said nothing.

A settlement worker called attention to the fact that the family lived in a depressed community with only drab surroundings, bad housing, and general tenement conditions. Dr. Rogers wondered whether there was evidence of malnutrition. A young college student with a smattering of Freudian lingo explained that it was a clear case of psychopathic stealing caused by sex repression. One man, who, Alison noticed, always found explanations on lower levels and was wont to flaunt a sophisticated air, pushed all these suggestions aside and said it was just a case of being "boy crazy." Alison wondered at the time whether there was any connection between this and the stories he was hearing about this man.

Yes, there could be no doubt that there was a great truth in the professor's dictum, so far as case conferences are concerned. We all necessarily judge others against the backgrounds of our own personalities and experiences. This makes the case conference no less valuable, much more of value, indeed. For they help the worker bringing in the case to correct her own judgment by those of others, and thus to eliminate more of her own personal element.

"Our judgments of others are projections of ourselves!" Then they are revealing concerning ourselves!

That made Alison feel quite humble that morning, as he recalled some of his own judgments hastily passed on others. How they revealed himself to himself, as he now considered them objectively! He was dismayed as he thought back over some of his earlier efforts and the way he had unconsciously displayed his own attitudes and other characteristics by the judgments he then passed on others. At the same time, now that he considers those judgments of his from this other viewpoint, he appreciates their value as means of knowing himself. Knowing these things about himself, he can hereafter better make allowances for them in his efforts to judge.

Like all other case workers, he must needs pass judgment on others and cannot escape his individual differentials in doing so. But he can undertake to understand them and make proper allowances for them. He wondered how widely social workers do this. Somehow, he could not escape the suspicion that much of the cocksureness he had sometimes found among them, much of their ex-cathedra finality in diagnosis, and occasional superciliousness toward him as only a preacher presuming to poach on their territories, had its rise in their never having passed through such meditations as his of this morning. Shades of Bobby Burns! "O, wud some power the giftie gie us, To see oursel's as ithers see us!"

"Our judgments of others are projections of ourselves!" Since that constitutes an important principle of diagnosis, he must get it across to his people. For Alison was always the true pastor; everything eventually came back to his work among his people. He would make this the basis for a sermon. A text came quickly to mind; "Thou that abhorest idols, dost thou commit sacrilege?" Paul may not have known our present-day psychological jargon, but here was an instance of keen psychological insight. Alison would enlarge on that text.

For no matter how inept any of us may be, we cannot escape the responsibility of making judgments of others, including their motives, desires, purposes. Business men have to do it every day. So do teachers, doctors, lawyers and church workers. He would try to interpret this principle to his people, so that they might more intelligently appraise their own judgments of others, and learn to judge them in part by the judgments they found them also passing. Verily, "Wherein thou judgest another, thou condemnest also thyself!" He recalled one of the rustic aphorisms he had heard in his boyhood from his farmer father: "If you find a man who thinks everybody is a thief, lock your chicken house door when he is around!"

"Our judgments of others are projections of ourselves!" Just what does that mean for the theories and hypotheses, the philosophies and theologies with which we approach the humans with whom we deal?

That set Alison to appraising those convictions on which he had been drawing as he continued the study of the dynamic forces in social and psychological experience. Recently he had been a bit disturbed when a psychologist had cynically remarked, "Your religion is just a matter of wishful thinking. You believe in a good God and in heaven because you want them to exist!" But this morning's musings suggested something else: Perhaps that was true of his thinking, and just as true of the thinking of the psychologist. After all, wishful thinking is no private preserve of religionists. Everybody does it, cannot escape it. Perhaps the psychologist does not believe in a holy and just God because there are reasons in his own life for wishing otherwise! Alison would not pass judgment on the sneering psychologist. But it did relieve him of any feeling of inferiority because of the remark.

In the same connection, he thought of the challenge sometimes expressed, more often implied, by non-religious persons, that there is nothing of real dynamic in religious experience as such. Presumably that thought has back of it the fact that they have never themselves experienced it in that way? He was reminded of the woman who once blurted out to the painter, Turner, regarding one of his masterpieces, "Really, Mr. Turner, I can't see anything worthwhile in that!" The great painter quietly replied, "Don't you wish you could?"

Then again, there were the differences of today in

theory in the fields of clinical psychology. How about the Adlerian thesis? May it be that men whose own emotional experiences in childhood were fraught with frustrations are the more inclined to find the dread fear of inferiority generally among others in distress? Or the Freudians? No, he would not allow himself to believe their constant finding of a dominating sex urge back of every neurosis and problem of conduct, had its real explanation in their own experience. He knew and highly esteemed too many Freudians for that. Yet we do need to realize that none of us can entirely get away from our personal equations even in our philosophies and our theories in science. Particularly in psychology, no one can ever be absolutely objective. Every psychological theory has in it an element of the emotional experience of its formulator. Therefore Alison would not feel disturbed because some psychological investigator whose work he found otherwise valuable, did not espouse or see values in religion. That perhaps only indicated certain poverties or distortions in that man's own experience. He would take and use the values he found and add to them those others which his own increasing religious experience was demonstrating.

"Projections of ourselves!" What responsibility that suggests! Alison recalled what had once been said about the remarkable successes of the late Weir Mitchell in psychotherapy: "The chief thing in the technique of Weir Mitchell was Weir Mitchell!" Alison, himself, was undertaking to bring a unique contribution from religion into the lives of others;

then, how much that contribution must depend on the reality and depth of his own religious life!

That thought drove him to his knees.

Seven years! Meditation over them had been so valuable to Alison that morning, why would it not be of equal value to bring them to the extended attention of his people by a proper observance of the anniversary of that Sunday when he had first launched the proposal for a different program?

His own people: it was they whom he would try to interest in this anniversary observance, not the general outside public. He still avoided publicity, particularly the kind which might direct attention to the experimental and novel features of his work and embarrass any in the community by seeming to hold them up as a sort of guinea pigs in a church experiment. But he did want his people to find the encouragement he himself was experiencing by looking back over those years and seeing the progress that had been made. Those who had been long with the church would appreciate the visible progress in the changed character of its program; those who had come in later years would likewise appreciate the differences which had attracted them when other churches had failed to interest them. Among them all would be many who would know from their own experiences how the clinical approach in Second Church had enabled them to find adjustments in their own lives, and had made living abundantly worthwhile.

He was tremendously in earnest. Just because he

was so much in earnest, he was not particularly interested in what might be said about him and his efforts elsewhere. Particularly was he not thinking in terms of how it might enhance his personal prestige and, perhaps, open doors to him in some larger field. His one concern was the effectiveness of what he was doing there.

Nevertheless, just because the work was succeeding there, it did attract attention. It attracted attention to him also, and approaches had been made to him to consider going to other churches. This he refused to do. Calls began coming for him to make addresses at all sorts of gatherings on the new plan of work. But he accepted very few. Running around to all sorts of meetings took entirely too much time from his work itself. Other ministers, coming to learn from his experience what might be of help to them in their own parishes, were always welcome. But as to all sorts of clubs and tea parties where men or women were wont to gather in what seemed to him much like the practice of the Athenians of whom Paul said they "spend their time in nothing else than either to tell or to hear some new thing," well, Alison felt that he had more important work to do than feed their curiosity and enjoy their plaudits. He was too much absorbed in making history to spend time talking about it.

As he had anticipated also, publicity attracted attention in other quarters where there were those who seriously questioned the policy of the church engaging in an extensive program of case work.

Rather sharp criticism came from a medical man

who was quite disturbed over some of the cases with which Alison was dealing, in which there was marked emotional disturbance. He insisted that this was the field of the physician, particularly the psychiatrist, and nobody else had any business undertaking to deal with such cases, certainly not a minister. There was even a suggestion that Alison was presuming to practice medicine without a license. Quite widespread talk had started in the community, so much indeed, that Alison considered it serious enough to bring the matter up at a meeting of his workers.

Dr. Rogers, who was one of those present said, "Forget it! Don't let some jealous little pill-roller, who is afraid you'll take a few dollars from him, worry you!" "But," said Alison, "I have not practiced psychiatry." "Of course you haven't," replied Dr. Rogers. "Not a bit more than a mother, who ties up her boy's cut toe or gives her girl some treatment for a cold, is practicing medicine.

"The trouble with some men in my profession is that they do not know enough themselves about these psycho-genetic disturbances. They got very little of it in medical school and too many of them are thinking all the time in terms of purely physical sources. I was in a group recently where I heard one of the leading diagnosticians in the country, a man on the staff of one of our greatest hospitals, make this statement: 'I will say on the basis of thirty-five years diagnostic experience that at least forty per cent of the sicknesses from which people suffer and die, are finally of psychic and not physical causation. More than that, I am convinced that religion can and should be used as one of the most useful therapeutic agents in that field.'

"I want to say," continued Rogers, "that my own experience leads me to the same conclusions. That's one reason I have been so interested in what our pastor has started here. Moreover, we need to realize that, just as in the physical field where I work, for every case of sickness severe enough to have the patient sent to the hospital for treatment by some specialist, there are forty cases of sore thumbs and headaches that the mothers take care of at home, just so it is here. In the matter of these emotional up-sets, a very large part of them are not only of mental origin, they are of spiritual origin. Something gets wrong in conduct, some unchristian attitude develops, and as a result the person is emotionally disturbed. What that person needs most is not some medical man who may know mighty little about such matters. A minister with training and skill, like our pastor, can do a far better job. If there is evidence of anything of the serious nature of a psychosis, he, of course, would not try to treat that. But he knows enough about it to detect symptoms of that kind of a case and bring it to our attention. Far from being a competitor of ours, I think he is a mighty valuable helper."

Dr. Roger's judgment on a question like this would of course be final with that group. They knew him as an efficient practitioner who stood high with his own profession, despite the seemingly harsh way in which he had just criticized some of them. Nevertheless, Alison took pains to make it very plain that none of their workers were to undertake in any way to make medical diagnoses or undertake any medical work themselves, or to assume that he would do so. He did think that he knew enough about emotional disturbances to perceive when the services of physician or psychiatrist were needed, and he would never presume to proceed otherwise in such a case. In the case of Roxanna, for instance, he had proceeded only in cooperation with Dr. Rogers, who had brought him into it. As time went on and the work of Second Church developed, the medical men in the community came to understand the real nature of Alison's work and to speak of it with appreciation. Not a few instances had occurred, in more recent years, in which physicians had sought the assistance of Alison and his helpers in dealing with situations developing in their own practice.

Another quarter in which it was found that the new program of the church would have to be interpreted, was with the social agencies.

While criticism from this quarter was not outspoken, Alison knew there was some uneasiness there. In some instances, he realized it rose in part out of uncertainties on the part of some of the agencies regarding their own future fields of service. This was particularly true of some which in former years had dispensed large amounts of material aid to those in economic distress, and in recent years had seen the development of newer policies whereby nearly all of this material aid is now supplied from tax supported sources. This raised a serious question regarding their own future functions. Case work now in many instances was of much the same kind as Second Church was undertaking; personal counseling, adjustment of family difficulties, assistance to physician and law officer in cases of neurotic sickness or problems of behavior. Jewish cases of this kind had for many years been taken care of generally by Jewish agencies. The Catholics are actively bringing their charity programs into line with modern scientific procedures, so that they are likely soon to take over the cases among their own people. If now the Protestant churches should do the same, what would it mean to the social agencies?

Alison was satisfied that this work would not displace the social agencies. And he took particular pains to have the social workers understand this also. He realized it would mean some changes in their programs, but they had long been used to that; they always assumed the character of their work would constantly change with changing conditions. But he had no intention of trying to turn history backwards, and have the church again assume responsibilities which since the Protestant reformation had increasingly been turned over to state and other agencies. What concerned him most was not what they were trying to do more or less well, but the great areas of need nobody was reaching. Here was the tragedy of it all. There are always many types of need which, in their very nature, are not going to be available for the social agency, and many of them are precisely the ones into which the church can most readily enter. On the other hand, there will always be tasks calling for the expert services of the skilled specialist in various kinds of social work, and the churches, in proportion as they develop intelligent case work programs of their own, will be making increasing use of these.

A third quarter from which suspicions and sometimes criticism had been voiced—and this particularly grieved Alison—was other churches. It was even hinted that Second Church was trying to pull their people away from them.

Regarding the Jews and Catholics, of whom there were not a few in the community, Alison had realized from the first that he must have a clearly understood policy. This, he felt, had been pretty effectively accomplished. He had made it quite explicit that he was not trying to pull any of those people away from their traditional affiliations. But if he, or any of his people, could at any time be of help to any such in really spiritual things, they would be only too happy to do so. After all, what we want to do, is to help one another into more wholesome relations with God and our fellowmen; the matter of what institutional connections they shall thereafter use for conserving these results is secondary. Of course, in case any of these people became dissatisfied with their former church connections, and felt that their religious interests could be better conserved by affiliating with Second Church, they were to feel that they would be welcome. But that was always a matter for them to decide. This policy seemed to have been generally satisfactory, and the relations with Jews and Catholics had been uniformly congenial.

With other Protestant churches, however, the experience had not been as gratifying. Why was it that brethren in the ministry so often were disturbed with fears that some other minister was trying to wean away their people? Why should one ever try to do so? Alison felt that it connoted an entirely wrong idea of our Christian objective, as though Christian accomplishment consisted in building up an institution, in getting people to enter and thus strengthen an institution, in glorifying a local church as an institution. After all, his Lord had never organized any church. Of course we need the Church; Alison never doubted that. We need the Church to conserve religion, just as we need the school to conserve education and the state to conserve the public order. But to place such emphasis on the Church that one measures his successes as a pastor by building it up as an institution, rather than by the individual souls which through his work and through the Church have been brought into the fuller joys of a deep religious experience and thereby a well adjusted life, well, Alison simply could not think in such terms. Of course, there was the economic side; he did not forget that. Fortunately for Second Church, it had some endowment, not enough to embarrass it by too much economic ease, but enough to relieve it from the anxieties which he realized beset some others whose pastors were worried constantly with problems of mere sustenance. Perhaps that was one reason some of them were so loath to give up a member, even on removal from their community. Pastors may decry economic determinism as a philosophy of life, but it does sometimes seem to warp not a little their own programs and attitudes.

As time went on, however, uncertainties in this regard also largely disappeared. Second Church had enjoyed a substantial growth and there was no longer any suggestion from anywhere about moving it away. The attendance at its services were little index to the outreach of its activities. The building had become the central operating plant of an organized enterprise involving many types of human service throughout the week at the hands of many workers. The church school had taken on much of the transformed character which had been projected some years before. A spiritual health clinic was maintained in the church, with particular attention to childhood. Mothers brought their children for examination, diagnostic tests, and prescription for their spiritual nurture and for dealing with their behavior problems. As a result, religious education was being increasingly accepted as primarily a responsibility of parents and home. Evangelism was ever to the fore, but as the spiritual therapy whereby sick souls were to be helped into life everlasting. Even revivalism had its place in the program; revivalism in the sense of occasional seasons of special consultation and prayer for the re-quickening and deepening of the religious experience and assurance of all.

With the coming of autumn the church made preparations to observe the seventh, the sabbatical anniversary of that historic Sunday when Alison had challenged them to join him in this proposed new endeavor. The preparations themselves were of value. They turned attention to the changes and progress that had come, and lent new courage as people talked together about the successes enjoyed. Of course, there had been disappointments and failures. Otherwise the experience would not have been true to life as they had known it. And these had only emphasized more those successes that were attained.

When the anniversary day came, there was an appropriate program climaxed by a surprise to the pastor which touched him deeply. There had been a resumé of the seven years' work, a comparison of the present with the former community outreach of the church, a renewing of fellowships with various ones who had returned for the day. The surprise came when the chairman of the official board asked for the privilege of making an announcement. He began by recalling that the sabbatical seventh year in Israel included, among other things, releases and readjustment. He stated that friends of the pastor had provided a special fund which he now had the privilege of handing to him, and the Official Board had voted him a special vacation to be taken at whatever time during the coming year he might choose, when he might fulfill a desire they knew he had entertained for some time, to make some studies of enterprises elsewhere from which suggestions might be obtained for still further enriching his future work at Second Church.